VISUAL QUICKSTART GUIDE

PageMill

FOR MACINTOSH

Maria Langer

Peachpit Press

Visual QuickStart Guide

PageMill for Macintosh

Maria Langer

Peachpit Press
2344 Sixth Street
Berkeley, CA 94710
800/283-9444
510/548-4393
510/548-5991 (fax)

Find us on the World Wide Web at: http://www.peachpit.com

Peachpit Press is a division of Addison Wesley Longman

Editors: Jeremy Judson and Nancy Davis
Copy Editor: Terry Wilson
Technical Editor: John Pirone
Cover Design: The Visual Group
Production: Maria Langer

Colophon

This book was created with QuarkXPress 3.31 on a Macintosh IIcx (yes, really!) and a Power Macintosh 7100/66. The fonts used were Charlotte, Charlotte Sans, and Corinthian Bold from Letraset.

ISBN 0-201-88661-8

9 8 7 6 5 4 3 2 1

Printed and bound in the United States of America

Dedication

To Bernard J. David,
with thanks.

Thanks!

To Jeremy Judson, Ted Nace, and the rest of the people at Peachpit Press for giving me the chance to show off my PageMill and Web publishing skills.

To Terry Wilson, for sharp-eyed copy editing and a seemingly endless stream of faxes marked "B.F."

To John Pirone, for making sure all the numbered steps, tips, and illustrations on these pages were correct.

To the developers of PageMill, for making such an easy-to-use Web publishing tool for Macintosh users.

And to Mike, for moral support and understanding.

http://www.intac.com/~gilesrd/

TABLE OF CONTENTS

Chapter 2: **Text Entry & Editing Basics**

Chapter 5: Working with Graphic Images

Chapter 7: Creating Forms

Chapter 9: Testing & Enhancing Pages

Appendix A: Menus & Command Key Equivalents

INTRODUCTION TO WEB PUBLISHING

Before You Begin...

If buying PageMill was your first big step into the realm of World Wide Web publishing, stop right here. There may be gaps in your understanding of the Web and how it works. It's a good idea to fill those gaps with basic background information before you go any further.

This introductory chapter was written for people who are brand new to the Internet and the World Wide Web. It explains what the Internet and World Wide Web are. It tells you about HTML and how it is interpreted by a special kind of software called a Web browser. It explains what PageMill does for you so you know exactly why you should be glad you use it. Finally, it provides a list of things to keep in mind when planning your Web site. All along the way, it defines important terms that will be used throughout this book.

You won't find many pictures in this introduction, but you will find lots of good, useful information. If you're new to the Internet or Web publishing, don't skip this introduction. The few minutes you spend here could save you hours in the future.

About the Internet

The Internet is a global network of computers. It's a lot like the network you might find in an office environment—but instead of the networked computers being separated by walls or cubicle partitions, they may be separated by miles, mountains, and oceans.

The Internet has been around since the 1960s, so it isn't new. What is new, however, is the boom in Internet interest and access. More people access the Internet today than ever before. And with access getting cheaper and easier all the time, it looks like the Internet will continue to grow long into the future.

The Internet offers access to many features. Here are just a few that interest most Internet users:

- **E-mail.** Electronic mail makes it possible to exchange written messages with other people all over the world, quickly and cost effectively.
- **Software.** FTP (file transfer protocol) sites offer the latest and greatest shareware and freeware files.
- **Discussion groups.** Newsgroups and mailing lists let participants join in topical discussions with people who share their interests.
- **"Published" Information.** Gopher, WAIS, and World Wide Web servers make it possible to publish and retrieve information from a wide variety of sources.

✔ Tip

- A lot of people think the phrase *World Wide Web* is the same as *Internet*. This isn't true. The World Wide Web is only part of the Internet. The Internet is far more than just the World Wide Web.

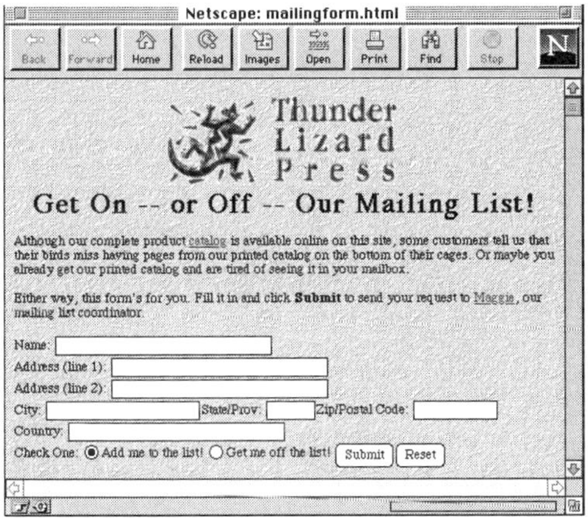

Figure 1. *This simple Web page, which was created with PageMill and is displayed here with Netscape Navigator, includes formatted text, graphics, hypertext links (underlined), and a form.*

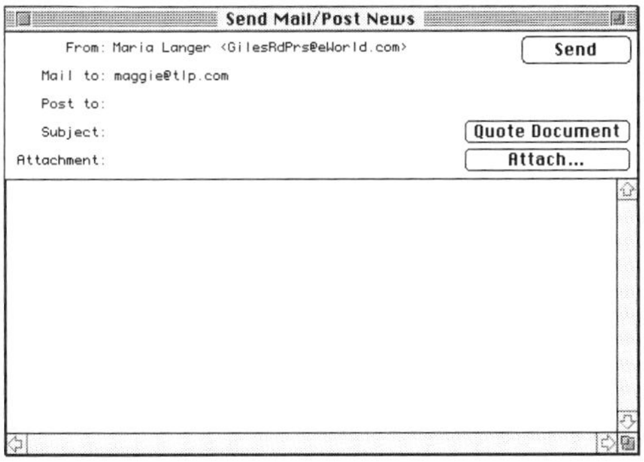

Figure 2. *Clicking a text or graphic link can display another page, download a file, or open a mail form like this one in Netscape Navigator.*

About the World Wide Web

The World Wide Web is the fastest growing part of the Internet. Often the first part of the Internet that new users explore, its popularity is due primarily to its graphic user interface and ease of use.

A Web *page* (see **Figure 1**) may include any combination of the following elements:

- **Formatted text.** Headings, bold and italic styles, indented lists, and other kinds of formatting can make text easier and more interesting to read.
- **Graphics.** Whether images, colorful lines, or background patterns, graphics can make pages visually appealing or share information that cannot be expressed in words.
- **Hypertext links.** Clicking a text or graphic link can display another page, download a file, or open a mail form (see **Figure 2**).
- **Forms.** Edit boxes, radio buttons, check boxes, and pop-up menus are some of the form elements that can collect information from a Web page viewer.

Each week, thousands of new pages appear on the World Wide Web. Web *publishers* include:

- Major corporations interested in global exposure.
- Small, medium, and large businesses interested in advertising (and selling) products and services.
- Individuals interested in sharing information about themselves.

The truth is, *anyone* can publish on the World Wide Web. If you've got something to say, the Web is a good place to say it—especially if you're ready for millions of people to get your message.

About HTML

One of the benefits of publishing on the World Wide Web is that Web pages can be read by any kind of computer using any kind of Web browser. (I tell you more about browsers on the next page.) This is possible through the use of a programming language called HyperText Markup Language (HTML). Plain text documents written with HTML codes can be interpreted by Web browsers, which display the codes as formatted text and graphics.

Figure 3 shows an example of what the HTML document for the simple Web page in **Figure 1** looks like. If you look closely, you can find and read the text that appears on the page. Everything else is an HTML markup code or tag that tells a Web browser how to format text, where to find graphics, and how to make form elements.

Fortunately, you don't need to deal with HTML codes. PageMill writes the codes for you automatically as you enter and format text, graphics, links, and form elements. It doesn't even show the codes to you.

mailingform.html

```
<HTML>
<HEAD>
  <TITLE></TITLE>
</HEAD>
<BODY
BACKGROUND="/Teeny/More%20Documents/gilesrd/mlanger/images/background.gif">
<FORM ACTION="default.cgi" ENCTYPE="x-www-form-encoded" METHOD="POST">
<H1><CENTER><IMG SRC="images/image4.gif" WIDTH="221" HEIGHT="87" ALIGN=middle
NATURALSIZEFLAG="0"><BR>
Get On -- or Off -- Our Mailing List!</CENTER>
</H1>
Although our complete product <A HREF="default.html">catalog</A> is available online on this
site, some customers tell us that their birds miss having pages from our printed catalog on
the bottom of their cages. Or maybe you already get our printed catalog and are tired of seeing
it in your mailbox.<BR>
<BR>
Either way, this form's for you. Fill it in and click <B>Submit</B> to send your request to <A
HREF="mailto:maggie@tlp.com">Maggie</A>, our mailing list coordinator.<BR>
<BR>
Name: <INPUT NAME="name" TYPE="text" SIZE="30"><BR>
Address (line 1): <INPUT NAME="name" TYPE="text" SIZE="30"><BR>
Address (line 2): <INPUT NAME="name" TYPE="text" SIZE="30"><BR>
City: <INPUT NAME="name" TYPE="text" SIZE="21">State/Prov: <INPUT NAME="name"
TYPE="text" SIZE="6">Zip/Postal Code: <INPUT NAME="name" TYPE="text" SIZE="11"><BR>
Country: <INPUT NAME="name" TYPE="text" SIZE="30"><BR>
Check One: <INPUT TYPE="radio" VALUE="radio" NAME="radio1088232"
CHECKED="true">Add me to the list! <INPUT TYPE="radio" VALUE="radio"
NAME="radio1088232">Get me off the list!  <INPUT NAME="name" TYPE="submit"
VALUE="Submit"><INPUT NAME="name" TYPE="reset" VALUE="Reset"><BR>
</FORM>
</BODY>
</HTML>
```

Figure 3. *Here's what's hidden behind the Web page in Figure 1. It's the HTML code written automatically by PageMill, displayed here in a SimpleText document window.*

✔ Tips

- PageMill supports HTML version 2 codes, along with some Netscape extensions. Appendix D lists the codes PageMill supports, as well as some commonly-used codes it doesn't support. It also explains what happens when you use PageMill to open a document that includes unsupported codes.
- If you know HTML, you can enter "raw HTML" codes in a PageMill document. If formatted correctly, these codes will be read and understood by browsers that support them. If PageMill does not support them, it will ignore them.
- If desired, you can open a document you created with PageMill with a text editor and enter or edit the HTML codes PageMill wrote for you.

About Web Browsers

Web browser software is what makes HTML code work. Programs like Netscape Navigator, NCSA Mosaic, and the Web browsers that come with America Online and eWorld software read HTML code, interpret it, and display it the way the Web page designer intended.

Well, not always. Unfortunately, not all Web browsers interpret HTML codes the same way. And not all Web browsers support all HTML codes. The only way to see exactly how your Web page will look when viewed with a specific browser is to open the page with that browser.

The good news is that PageMill supports codes that are recognized and properly interpreted (or ignored) by all Web browsers. Its Preview view emulates a Web browser so what you see on screen will closely resemble what the people who view the page on the Web will see with their browsers.

✔ Tips

- Each major computer platform—Macintosh, Windows, and UNIX—has its own collection of Web browsers. Because of this, your Web pages can look very similar from one platform to the next. This makes the Web a perfect cross-platform environment for sharing information—even if that information is accessible only within an organization's network and not the Internet.
- Throughout this book, the term Web browser refers to a *graphic* browser—one that is capable of displaying formatted text and graphics on Web pages. A *text* browser is another kind of browser that displays Web pages as unformatted text documents. Although text browser users will not see the graphics and formatting of your pages, they will see the textual content.

About Your Web Site

If you're creating a Web site from the ground up, you can create an effective site and save yourself a lot of aggravation by planning ahead. Here are a few things to consider:

- **What do you want your pages to look like?** If you plan on having multiple pages, you may want to use consistent formatting, colors, background patterns, logos, or other elements to give your site its own identity and set it apart from the others.
- **Will your pages be long or short?** Long pages make it possible to provide more information with fewer hits to the site. Short pages load more quickly. Each approach has its pros and cons.
- **Will your pages rely heavily on graphics?** Remember that not all people who browse the World Wide Web do so with graphic browsers. These people won't be able to see your pictures.
- **How do you want to organize your pages?** Create an outline showing the relationship between pages so you know how the pages will link to each other.
- **How do you want to store your pages and other files on disk?** Take advantage of the hierarchical file system to organize files in folders and subfolders.

These are just a few things to think about before you even launch PageMill. Browse the World Wide Web to see what other Web publishers are doing. Examine the sites that appeal to you and figure out what makes you like them more than others. Anyone can create Web pages, but it takes creativity and planning to put together *effective* Web pages—the ones people visit regularly and share with their friends.

GETTING STARTED WITH PAGEMILL

1

Introduction

PageMill is an Internet authoring tool that makes it easy to create Web pages. You can use PageMill's word processor-like interface and drag-and-drop editing techniques to enter, edit, and format Web pages, add graphics and links to other pages, and even create forms for gathering information from the Internet "surfers" who browse your pages. With PageMill, there's no need to struggle with complex HyperText Markup Language (HTML) codes. PageMill does all the HTML coding work for you, behind the scenes.

This Visual QuickStart Guide will help you master PageMill by providing step-by-step instructions, plenty of illustrations, and a generous helping of tips. Within these pages you'll find everything you need to know about PageMill—and more!

This book is designed for page-flipping. Use the thumb tabs, index, or table of contents to find the topics for which you need help. If you're brand new to PageMill, however, I recommend that you begin by reading at least this first chapter. In it, you'll find important introductory information about PageMill's interface and preference settings.

The World Wide Web has opened the world of publishing to anyone with something to say. PageMill is one of the best tools around to get your message out on the Web with the least amount of effort.

About Running PageMill

The PageMill installer places a number of files on your hard disk in a folder called PageMill™ Folder (see **Figure 1**). One of these files is the PageMill application.

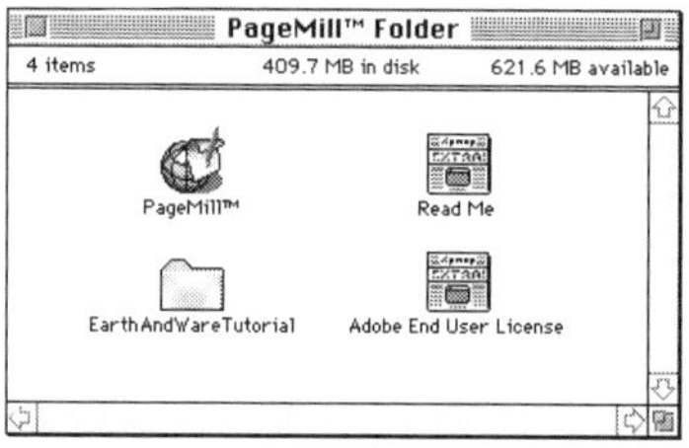

Figure 1. *Inside the PageMill™ Folder.*

To launch PageMill

1. Locate and open the PageMill™ Folder (see **Figure 1**).
2. Double-click the PageMill™ icon.

or

Double-click a PageMill document icon (see **Figure 2**).

Figure 2. *A PageMill document icon.*

The PageMill splash screen appears briefly (see **Figure 3**). When it disappears, you'll see PageMill's menu bar at the top of the screen (see **Figure 4**). If you launched PageMill by double-clicking a document icon, its document window appears.

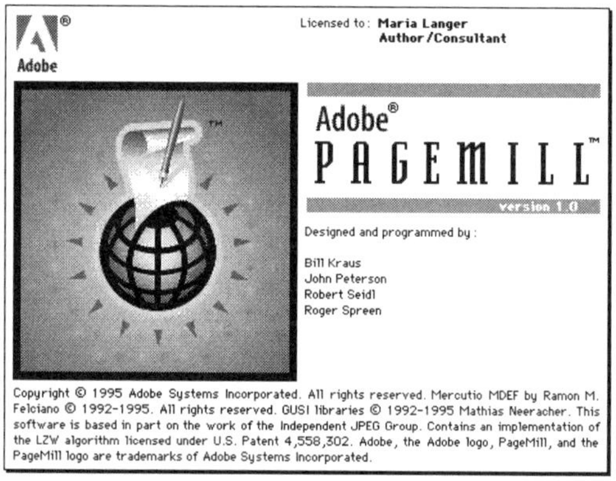

Figure 3. *A splash screen appears briefly when you launch PageMill.*

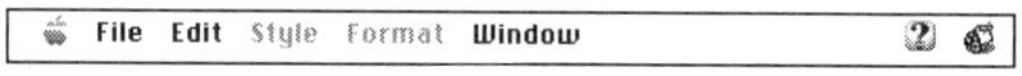

Figure 4. *PageMill's menu bar.*

✔ Tips

- The first time you launch PageMill, a registration screen appears (see **Figure 5**). You must enter your name, organization, and PageMill registration number in the appropriate edit boxes and click OK before you can proceed.
- When you launch PageMill by double-clicking its icon, it does not automatically create a new document.

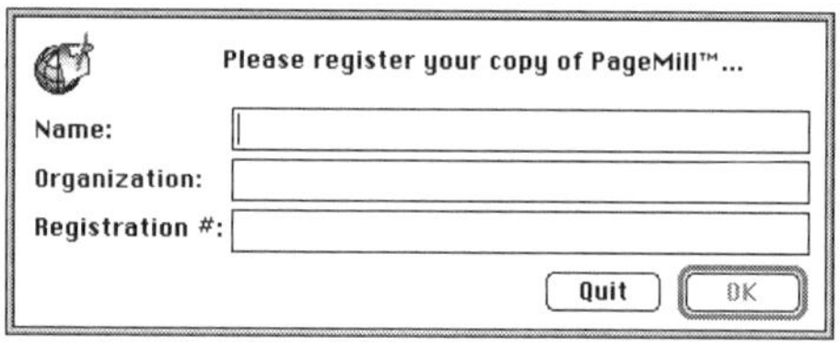

Figure 5. *The first time you use PageMill, you must provide registration information.*

To quit PageMill

Choose Quit from the File Menu (see **Figure 6**).

or

Press ⌘Q.

Figure 6. *To quit PageMill, choose Quit from the File menu.*

✔ Tip

- Closing all document windows is not the same as quitting the program. PageMill continues to run and take up RAM until you use its Quit command.

Figure 7. *Page or Edit view is where you create and edit Web pages.*

Figure 8. *Image view is where you create image maps and change the way images appear.*

Figure 9a. *In Page view, the Toggle Preview Mode button looks like this…*

Figure 9b. *… and in Preview view, the Toggle Preview Mode button looks like this.*

About PageMill's Views

PageMill offers three views or modes:

- Page (or Edit) view (see **Figure 7**) lets you create and edit Web pages. You'll work in Page view throughout this book.
- Preview view lets you see what your Web pages will look like on the World Wide Web and test any internal links you may have included on them. I tell you about previewing and testing pages in **Chapter 9**.
- Image view (see **Figure 8**) lets you create image maps and specify the way an image appears on a page. I tell you how to use Image view options in **Chapters 5** and **6**.

To toggle between Page & Preview views

Click the Toggle Preview Mode button in the upper right corner of the Page window (see **Figures 9a** and **9b**). The view and button icon change.

✔ Tip

- There are very subtle differences between the appearance of Page view and Preview view. You can always tell which view you're in by checking the Toggle Preview Mode button (see **Figures 9a** and **9b**).

To go to Image view

In Page view, double-click an image. The Image view window appears (see **Figure 8**).

✔ Tip

- You must be in Page view in order to switch to Image view by double-clicking an image.

About Page View Tools

In Page view, a button bar beneath the window's title bar (see **Figure 10**) offers easy access to a number of options and commands. I tell you about using these tools throughout this book.

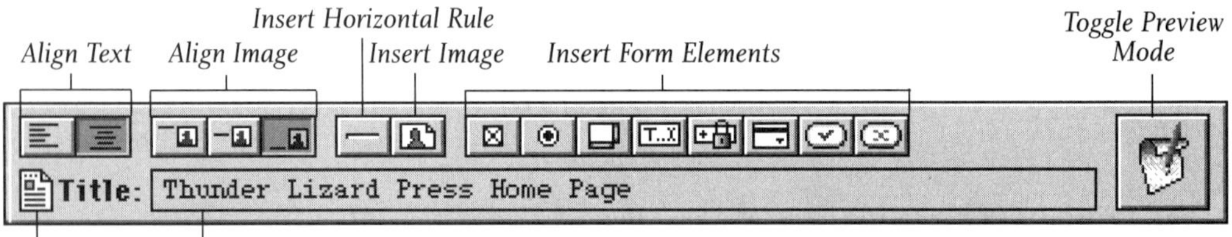

Figure 10. *Tools and buttons at the top of the PageMill window give you easy access to commands and other options.*

✔ Tip

- To learn what a button does, point to it with your mouse. The button name or description appears immediately to the left of the Toggle Preview Mode button (see **Figure 11**).

Figure 11. *Point to a button to learn what it is.*

About PageMill's Menus

Most of PageMill's commands are accessible through its menus. **Figures 12a** and **12b** illustrate two of PageMill's menus.

- A menu command that appears in gray cannot currently be selected.
- A menu command followed by an ellipsis (...) displays a dialog box.
- A menu command followed by a triangle has a submenu. The submenu displays additional commands when the main command is highlighted.
- A menu command followed by the ⌘ (Command key) symbol and one or more other symbols or letters can be chosen with a Command key equivalent. **Table 1** lists the symbols that appear on menus and their keyboard equivalents.
- A menu command preceded by a check mark has been "turned on."

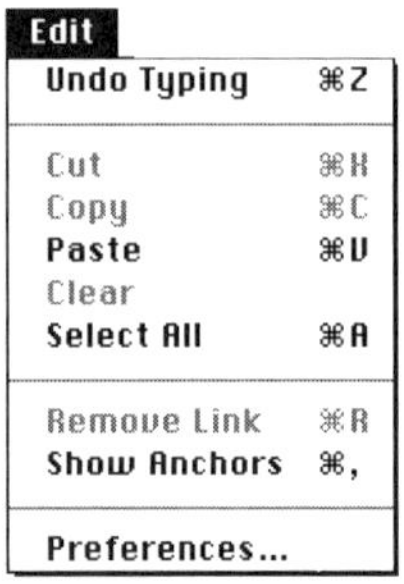

Figure 12a. *PageMill's Edit menu.*

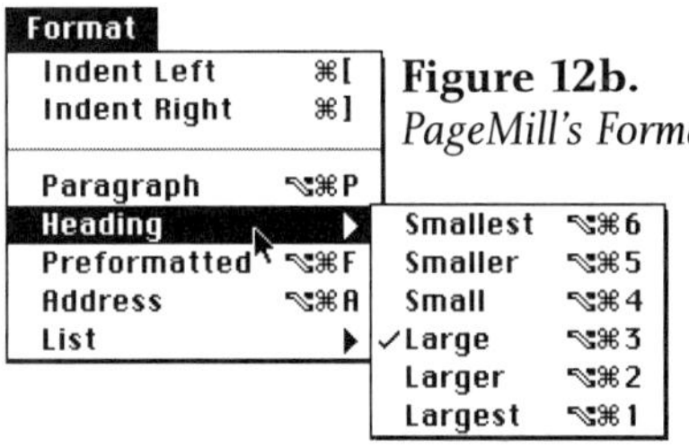

Figure 12b. *PageMill's Format menu.*

Menu Symbol	Keyboard Key
⌘	[⌘]
⌥	[Option]
⇧	[Shift]

Table 1. *Command key equivalent menu symbols and corresponding keyboard keys.*

To use a menu

1. Point to the menu from which you want to choose a command.
2. Press the mouse button and hold it down to display the menu.
3. Drag the mouse pointer down until the command you want is highlighted.
4. Release the mouse button. The command may blink before the menu disappears, confirming that it has been successfully selected.

✔ Tip

- If the command is on a submenu, display the submenu (see **Figure 12b**), then drag the mouse pointer to the right and down until the submenu command is highlighted.

To use a Command key equivalent

1. Hold down the modifier key(s) (normally [⌘], but sometimes also [Shift] and/or [Option]).
2. Press the letter, number, or punctuation key for the equivalent.

For example, as the Format menu indicates (see **Figure 12b**), the Command key equivalent for the Address command is ⌥⌘A. To use this shortcut, hold down the [Option] and [⌘] keys and press [A].

✔ Tip

- **Appendix A** at the end of this book includes a complete listing of all Command key equivalents.

About the Pasteboard

The Pasteboard (see **Figure 14**) is a place within PageMill where you can store frequently-used Web page elements like text and graphics.

For example, say you include your company logo on each Web page you create. If you store it on the Pasteboard, it will be within mouse pointer reach each time you create a new page.

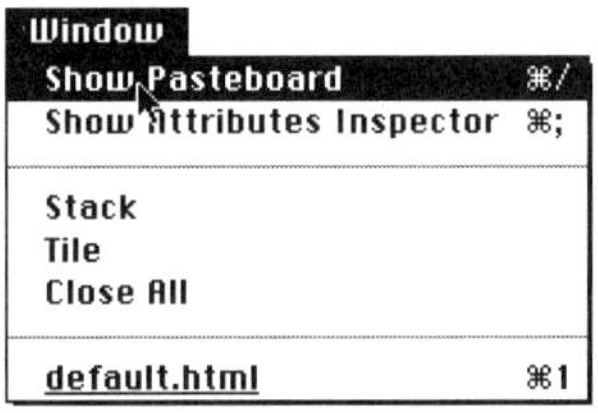

Figure 13. *Choose Show Pasteboard from the Window menu to display the Pasteboard while you work.*

✔ Tips

- Although the Pasteboard has only five pages, you can store more than one item on each page.
- I provide details on adding items to the Pasteboard, using items stored on the Pasteboard, and removing items from the Pasteboard in **Chapters 2** and **5**.

To show the Pasteboard

Choose Show Pasteboard from the Window menu (see **Figure 13**).

or

Press ⌘/.

The Pasteboard appears (see **Figure 14**).

To hide the Pasteboard

Choose Hide Pasteboard from the Window menu.

or

Press ⌘/.

or

Click the Pasteboard's close box (see **Figure 14**).

The Pasteboard disappears.

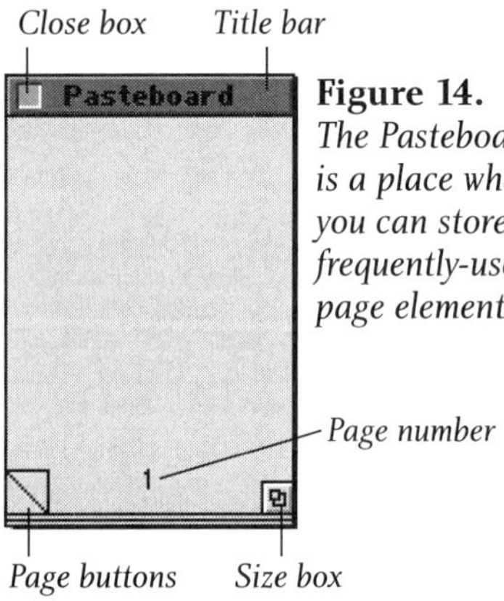

Figure 14. *The Pasteboard is a place where you can store frequently-used page elements.*

✔ Tips

- To move the Pasteboard, drag it by its title bar.
- To resize the Pasteboard, drag its size box. When you release the mouse button, the Pasteboard is resized.
- To change Pasteboard pages, click one of the page button triangles. Clicking the top triangle switches to the next page; clicking the bottom triangle switches to the previous page.

Using the Pasteboard

About the Attributes Inspector

The Attributes Inspector (see **Figure 16**) is a palette full of options you can use to set attributes for an entire page, selected text, or selected objects.

✔ Tips

- The Attributes Inspector will only offer options when a page is in Page view. When no page is open or when the open page is in Preview view, the Attributes Inspector window is empty.
- I tell you how to use the Attributes Inspector's options throughout this book.

To show the Attributes Inspector

Choose Show Attributes Inspector from the Window menu (see **Figure 15**).

or

Press [⌘;].

The Attributes Inspector appears (see **Figure 16**).

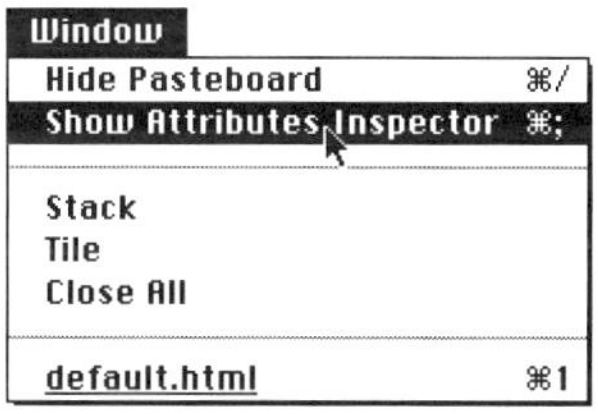

Figure 15. *Choose Show Attributes Inspector from the Window menu to display a palette of options while you work.*

✔ Tips

- To move the Attributes Inspector, drag it by its title bar.
- To switch between page, text, and object attributes, click the appropriate button bar button (see **Figure 16**).

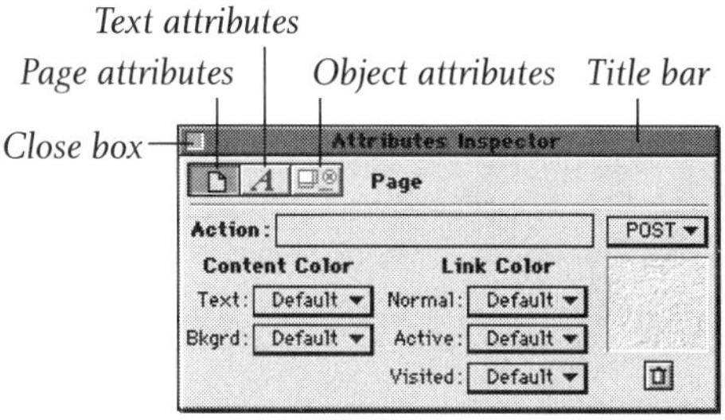

Figure 16. *The Page attributes of the Attributes Inspector.*

To hide the Attributes Inspector

Choose Hide Attributes Inspector from the Window menu.

or

Press [⌘;].

or

Click the Attributes Inspector's close box (see **Figure 16**).

Using the Attributes Inspector

About PageMill Preferences

PageMill's Preferences dialog box (see **Figure 18**) lets you specify settings that affect the way PageMill formats, saves, and names files.

To toggle the page flipping sound effect

1. Choose Preferences from the Edit menu (see **Figure 17**). The Preferences dialog box appears (see **Figure 18**).
2. Click the Page Flip Sound check box to toggle the setting on or off.
3. Click OK or press Return or Enter to accept your changes.

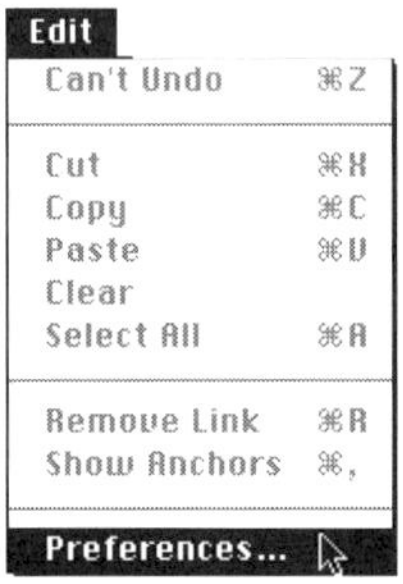

Figure 17. *To open the Preferences dialog box, choose Preferences from the Edit menu.*

To set line break format, file suffix, or map format options

1. Choose Preferences from the Edit menu (see **Figure 17**). The Preferences dialog box appears (see **Figure 18**).
2. Choose the appropriate format from the Line Breaks pop-up menu (see **Figure 19a**).

   or

   Choose the desired suffix from the File Suffix pop-up menu (see **Figure 19b**).

   or

   Choose the appropriate map format from the Map Format pop-up menu (see **Figure 19c**).
3. Click OK or press Return or Enter to accept your changes.

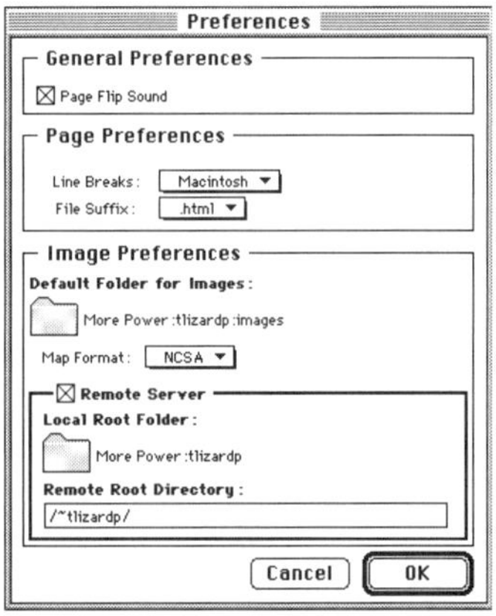

Figure 18. *The Preferences dialog box lets you specify settings that affect the way PageMill writes information to files.*

Figure 19a. *PageMill offers three line break format options,...*

Figure 19b. *...two file suffix options,...*

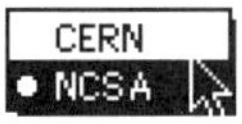

Figure 19c. *...and two map format options.*

✔ Tip

- Line break format, default file suffix, and map format preferences should be set according to the requirements of your Web server. If you're not sure what the correct settings are, ask your Webmaster or System Administrator.

To set the default image folder or local root folder

1. Choose Preferences from the Edit menu (see **Figure 17**). The Preferences dialog box appears (see **Figure 18**).
2. To set the path to the default image folder (the folder in which you will store image files and maps used in Web pages), click the folder icon beneath Default Folder for Images.

   or

   To set the path to the local root folder (the folder in which you will store completed Web pages), click the folder icon beneath Local Root Folder.

   An Open dialog box appears (see **Figure 20**).
3. Use the dialog box to locate and open the folder in which you want to store the images or completed pages.
4. Click the In Here button to set the path.
5. Click OK or press Return or Enter in the Preferences dialog box to accept your changes.

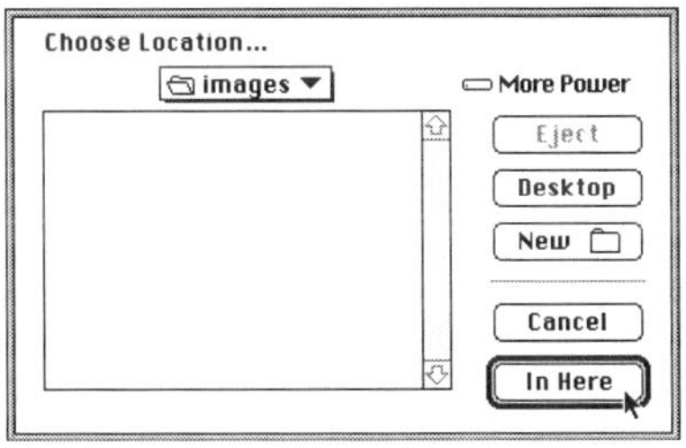

Figure 20. *To choose a default image folder or local root folder, use a specialized Open dialog box.*

To set the remote root directory

1. Choose Preferences from the Edit menu (see **Figure 17**). The Preferences dialog box appears (see **Figure 18**).
2. If necessary, turn on the Remote Server check box.
3. In the Remote Root Directory edit box, type in the complete path name for the root directory of the remote server. (If you're not sure what it is, ask your Webmaster or System Administrator.)
4. Click OK or press Return or Enter in the Preferences dialog box to accept your changes.

Setting Folder Preferences

✔ Tips

- Before you set PageMill folder preferences, create a folder on your hard disk for the storage of page and image files. Then, if preferences are properly set, PageMill's page names and references for linked pages will be correct.
- For best results, the default image folder should be inside the folder containing your completed Web pages.
- In order to set the local root folder path, you may have to turn on the Remove Server check box first.

TEXT ENTRY & EDITING BASICS 2

About Entering & Editing Text with PageMill

One of the best features of PageMill is its word processor-like interface. As you work with PageMill, you'll use the same techniques you use with your word processor. Here are some examples:

- Create, open, save, and print documents with commands under the File menu.
- Enter text by typing at an insertion point.
- Edit text by selecting and typing to replace or pressing [Delete] to delete.
- Cut, copy, and paste text to duplicate or move it.
- Use the Undo command to reverse your last action.
- Move, resize, and switch windows by dragging or clicking standard window parts.

In addition to these standard techniques, PageMill offers additional features and techniques that make it easy to enter and edit text in documents, including:

- Drag and drop text editing to move or copy text quickly.
- The Pasteboard to store items you use repeatedly.
- The Revert command to throw away all changes to an open document.

Best of all, at any time during the Web page creation process, you can click the Toggle Preview button to see how your page will look and work on the World Wide Web.

About Page Files

Each document you create with PageMill is a *page*. Don't let this familiar term fool you—a Web page can be as long or short as you like.

To create a new page

Choose New Page from the File menu (see **Figure 1**).

or

Press ⌘N.

An empty document window named *untitled.html* (or *untitled1.html*, etc.) appears (see **Figure 2**).

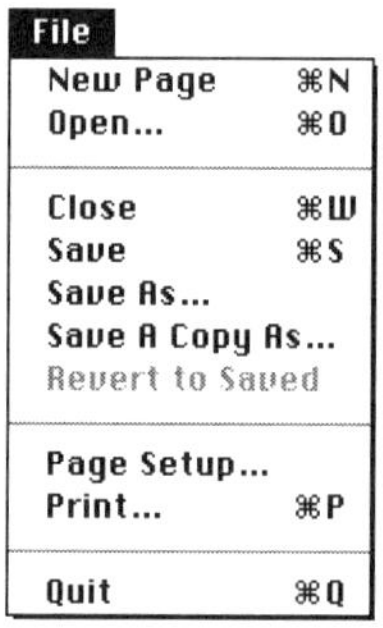

Figure 1. *The File menu offers commands to create new page files, open existing page files, and close page files.*

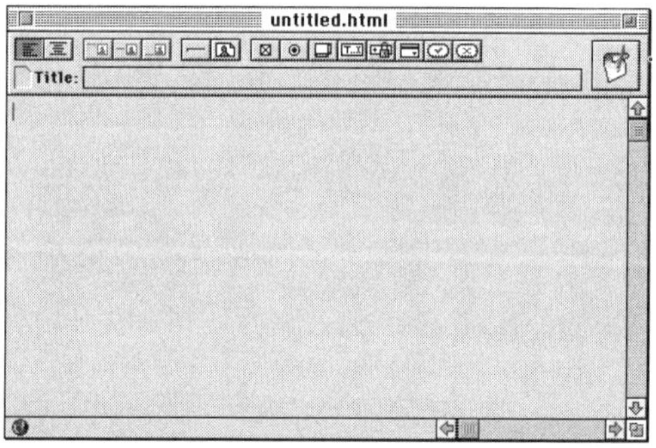

Figure 2. *When you use the New Page command, an "untitled" window appears.*

To open an existing page

1. Choose Open from the File menu (see **Figure 1**).

   or

   Press ⌘O.

   A standard Open dialog box appears (see **Figure 3**).
2. Locate and select the Web page document you want to open.
3. Click OK or press Return or Enter.

or

In the Finder, double-click the icon for the PageMill document you want to open. If PageMill isn't already running, this will launch it, too.

or

In the Finder, drag a Web page document icon onto the PageMill application icon. This is a good way to use PageMill to open a Web page created by another program.

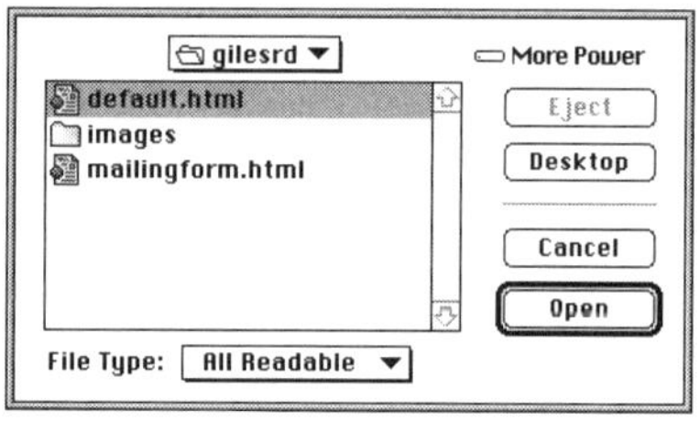

Figure 3. *Use the Open dialog box to open existing Web page files.*

✔ Tip

- When you open an existing page, PageMill displays it in Preview view. Click the Toggle Preview Mode button (see **Figure 4**) to switch to Edit view to make changes to the page.

Figure 4. *Click the Toggle Preview Mode button to edit pages you open.*

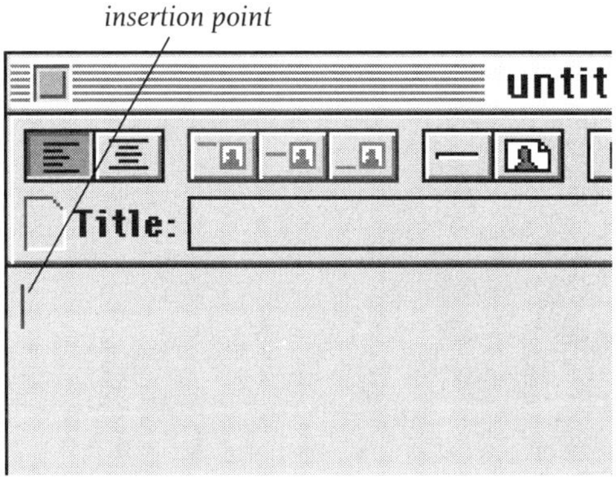

Figure 5. *The blinking insertion point indicates where the text you type will appear.*

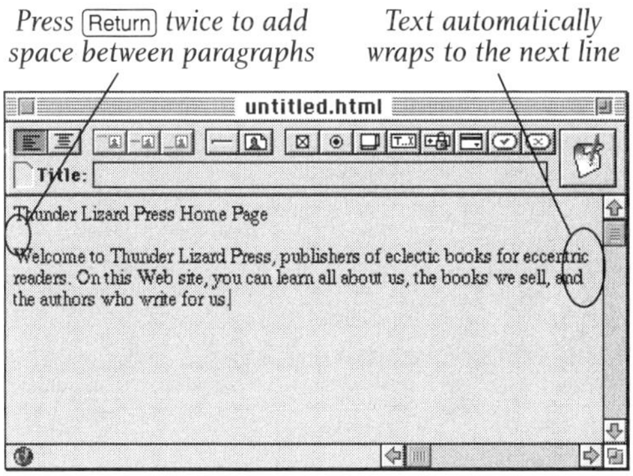

Figure 6. *The PageMill document window works just like a word processing document window.*

Character	Keystroke
<	Shift .
>	Shift ,
&	Shift 7
®	Option R
©	Option G

Table 1. *Keystrokes for some special characters supported by PageMill.*

About Entering Text

In most cases, text will form the basis of your Web page. Entering text in a PageMill document is as easy as entering it in any word processing document.

To enter text by typing

1. Position the blinking insertion point where you want the text to appear (see **Figure 5**) by clicking or using the arrow keys on your keyboard.
2. Type.

The text you type appears at the insertion point (see **Figure 6**).

✔ Tips

- It is not necessary to press Return at the end of each line. Text automatically wraps when it reaches the right side of the window (see **Figure 6**).
- Word wrap is determined by the width of the window.
- To add space between paragraphs, press Return twice. Each time you press Return you get a new, empty line (see **Figure 6**). Keep in mind, however, that not all browsers recognize two or more consecutive blank lines.

To enter special characters

Type the character you want.

Table 1 provides a list of some of the characters PageMill supports, along with the keys you press to type them.

✔ Tip

- "Special" characters are either not among the standard keyboard characters or reserved for use within HTML. PageMill automatically converts these characters to HTML codes so they can be used in Web pages and interpreted properly by Web browsers.

To enter text by opening a plain text document

1. Choose Open from the File menu (see **Figure 1**).

   or

   Press [⌘][O].
2. In the standard Open dialog box that appears (see **Figure 3**), make sure All Readable or TEXT is selected from the File Type pop-up menu (see **Figure 7**).
3. Select the file you want to open and click Open or press [Return] or [Enter].
4. If the file is not a Web page file, a dialog box appears, telling you that it does not contain any HTML tags (see **Figure 8**). Click Yes to open the file anyway.

The document opens in a PageMill window (see **Figure 9**). Although the original document may have included line breaks and other formatting options (see **Figure 10**), they are lost when the file is opened in PageMill. Use basic text insertion techniques (which are discussed on the next page) to rebreak lines and insert blank lines.

✔ Tip

- A better way to take the contents of a plain text file and turn it into a PageMill document is to open the text file, copy its contents, and then paste it into a new, empty PageMill document. Doing this carries forward the Return characters in the text. I tell you about using the Copy and Paste commands later in this chapter.

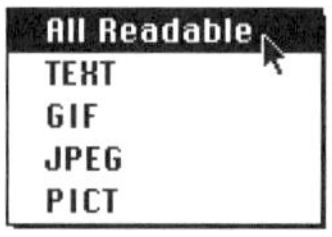

Figure 7. *To open a plain text file, make sure All Readable or TEXT is selected in the Open dialog box.*

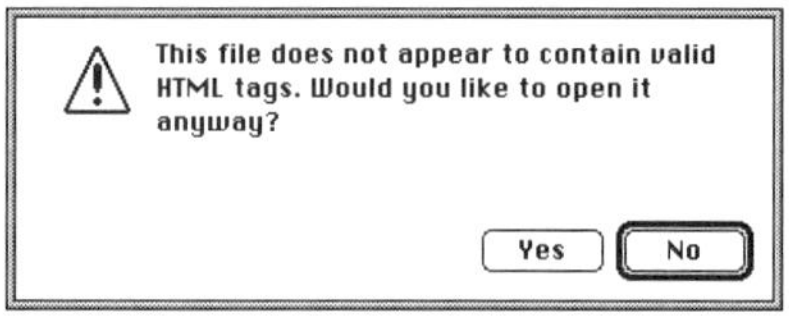

Figure 8. *If you try to open a document that does not contain HTML codes, a dialog box like this appears.*

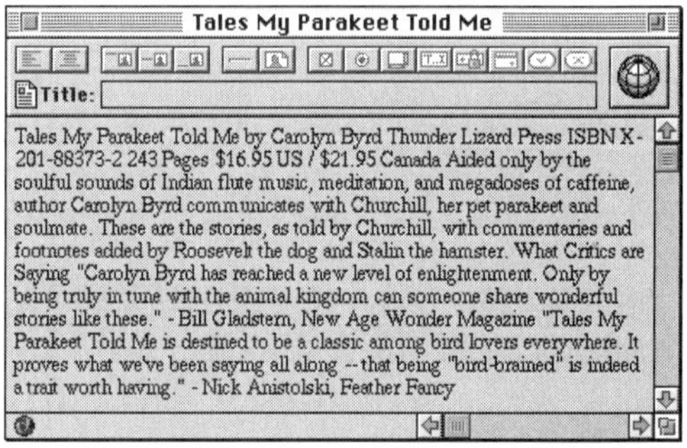

Figure 9. *When you open a plain text document, all formatting is lost…*

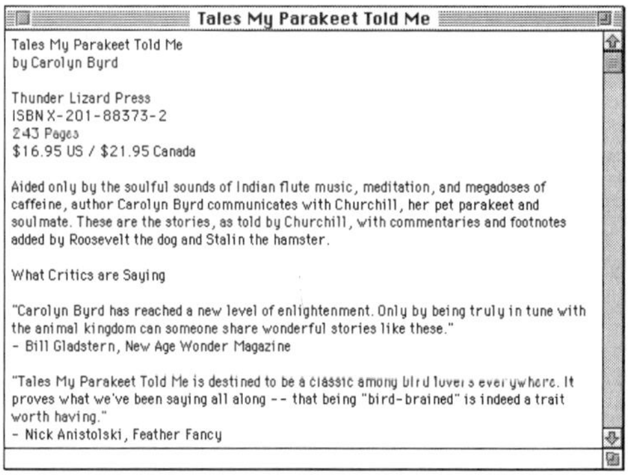

Figure 10. *…as you can see by comparing it to the original text file here.*

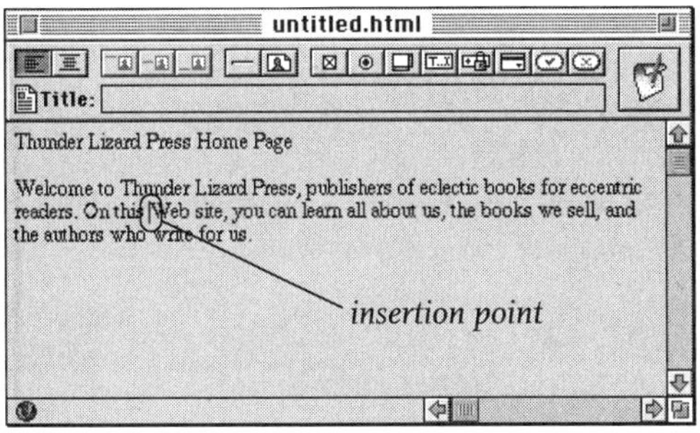

Figure 11. *To insert text, begin by positioning the insertion point…*

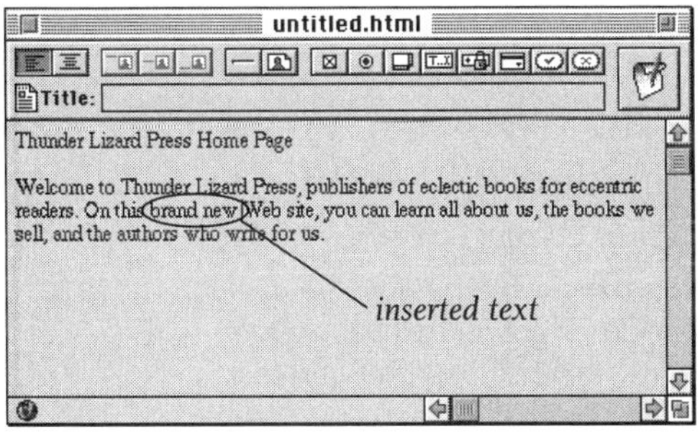

Figure 12. *…then type. The text you type is inserted and the text to the right of it moves to the right or down to make room for it.*

Figure 13. *To break a line, position the insertion point…*

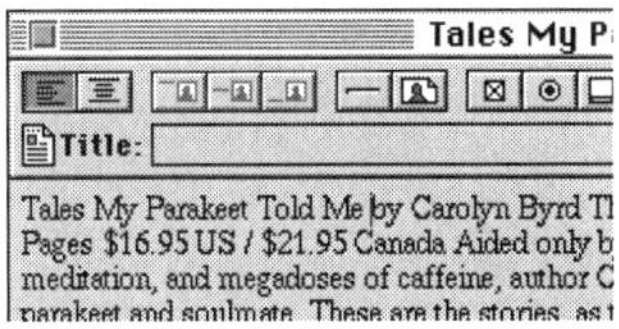

Figure 14. *…then press* Return.

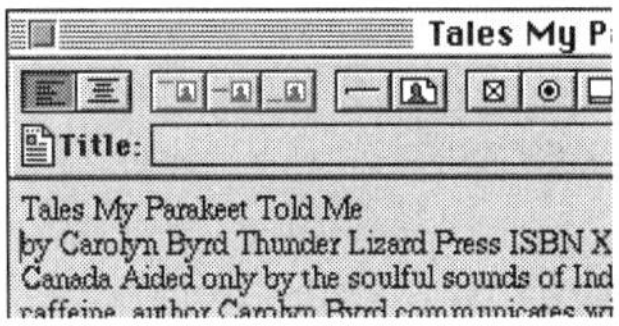

✔ Tip

- To remove a line break, position the insertion point at the beginning of the second line and press Delete to delete the Return character at the end of the previous line.

About Editing Text

Once text has been entered, it's easy to edit. As you might imagine, standard word processing techniques apply.

To insert text

1. Position the blinking insertion point where you want the text to appear (see **Figure 11**). You can do this by clicking or using the arrow keys.
2. Type.

Because PageMill uses an insertion cursor, text you type is inserted at the blinking insertion point (see **Figure 12**). Text to the right of or below the insertion point is pushed aside or down for the new text.

✔ Tip

- To break a line, position the insertion point before the character you want to appear on the next line (see **Figure 13**). Then press Return (see **Figure 14**).

To delete text

1. Position the blinking insertion point to the right of the character(s) you want to delete.
2. Press Delete to delete the character to the left of the insertion point. To delete multiple characters, just keep pressing Delete until they're all gone.

or

1. Select the text you want to delete. (I tell you how to select text on the next page.)
2. Press Delete.

   or

   Choose Clear from the Edit menu (see **Figure 20** on the next page).

To select text characters

1. Position the mouse pointer, which must look like an I-beam pointer (see **Figure 15**), at the beginning of the text you want to select.
2. Press the mouse button down and drag to the end of the text you want to select (see **Figure 16**). As you drag, text is selected.

or

1. Click at the beginning of the text you want to select to position the insertion point there (see **Figure 17**).
2. Hold down Shift and click at the end of the text you want to select (see **Figure 17**). The text between the first and second click is selected.

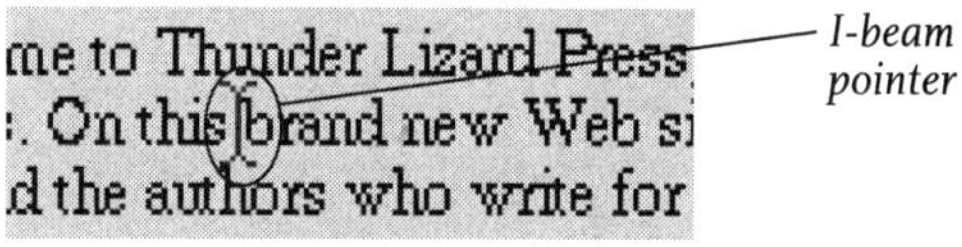

Figure 15. *Position the mouse pointer at the beginning of the text you want to select…*

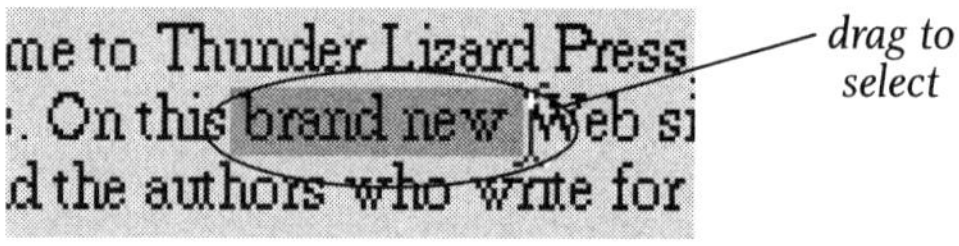

Figure 16. *…then drag to select the text.*

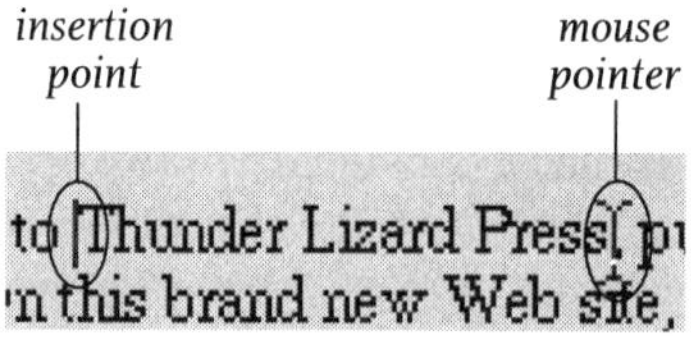

Figure 17. *Hold down* Shift *and click to select all text between the blinking insertion point and the mouse pointer.*

✔ Tip

- If the mouse pointer looks like an arrow pointer when you drag to select text using the first technique above, you probably already have text selected and will move it when you drag. Click once on any other text in the document window to clear the selection and try again.

To select a word

1. Position the mouse pointer, which must look like an I-beam pointer (see **Figure 18**), in the middle of a word you want to select.
2. Double-click. The entire word is selected and the mouse pointer turns into an arrow pointer (see **Figure 19**).

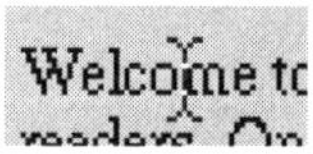

Figure 18. *Position the mouse pointer on the word…*

Figure 19. *…then double-click to select it.*

To select all document contents

Choose Select All from the Edit menu (see **Figure 20**).

or

Press ⌘A.

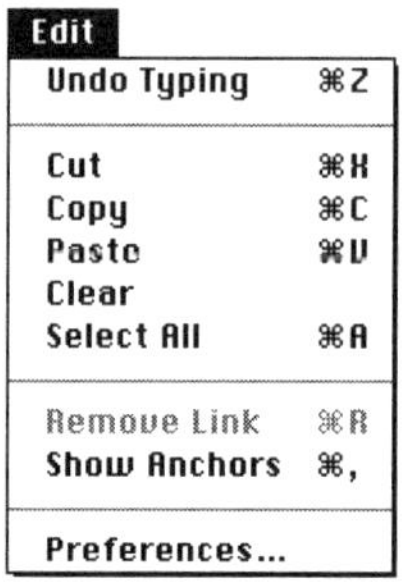

Figure 20. *The Edit menu includes a wide variety of commands for editing text.*

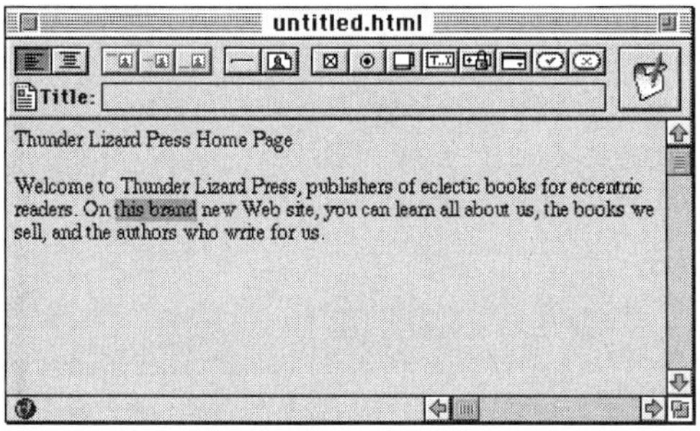

Figure 21. *To replace text, begin by selecting the text…*

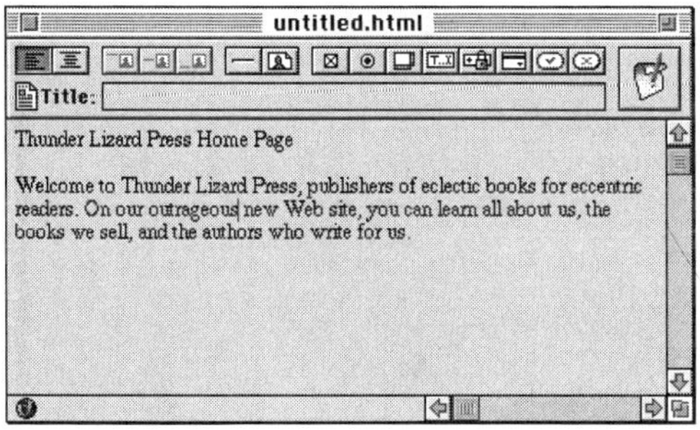

Figure 22. *…then just type. The new text replaces the selected text.*

To replace text

1. Select the text you want to replace (see **Figure 21**).
2. Type.

The text you type replaces whatever text was selected when you began typing (see **Figure 22**).

✔ Tips

- Pressing [Delete] or choosing Clear from the Edit menu (see **Figure 20**) while text is selected deletes the text by replacing it with nothing.
- You can also replace text by using the Paste command when text is selected. I tell you about the Paste command on the next few pages.
- If you accidentally replace text instead of inserting it, immediately use the Undo command, which I tell you about later in this chapter, to get back the original text.

To deselect text

Click once on any other text in the document window. The selection clears.

✔ Tip

- It's vital that no text is selected when you type if you want to insert (not replace) text. Make sure you know exactly where the insertion point is before typing. If text is selected, there won't be an insertion point. Remember, when text is selected, anything you type will overwrite the selected text.

About Copying & Moving Text

PageMill offers a variety of ways to copy and move text:

- The Copy and Paste commands let you copy text from one place and paste it in another.
- The Cut and Paste commands let you cut text from one place and paste it in another, thus moving the original text.
- Drag and drop text editing lets you move or copy selected text by simply dragging it.
- The Pasteboard lets you store text that you can drag into a document window.

To copy text with Copy & Paste

1. Select the text you want to copy (see **Figure 23**).
2. Choose Copy from the Edit menu (see **Figure 20**).

   or

   Press [⌘C].

   The text is copied to the Clipboard. It remains selected in the document.
3. Position the insertion point where you want the copied text to be inserted (see **Figure 24**).
4. Choose Paste from the Edit menu (see **Figure 20**).

   or

   Press [⌘V].

   A copy of the text in the Clipboard is pasted into the document at the insertion point (see **Figure 25**).

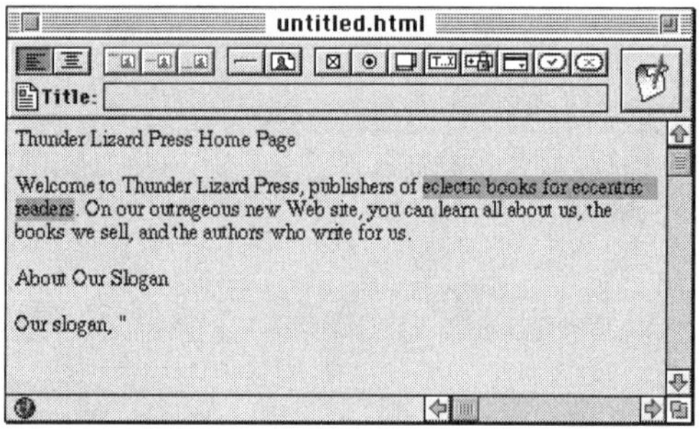

Figure 23. *To use the Copy or Cut commands, you must begin by selecting something.*

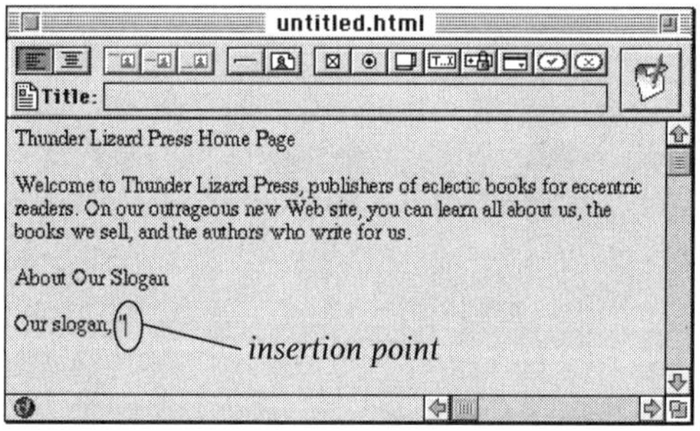

Figure 24. *Position the insertion point where you want a copy of the text in the clipboard to be pasted…*

Figure 25. *…so when you use the Paste command, the text is placed just where you want it.*

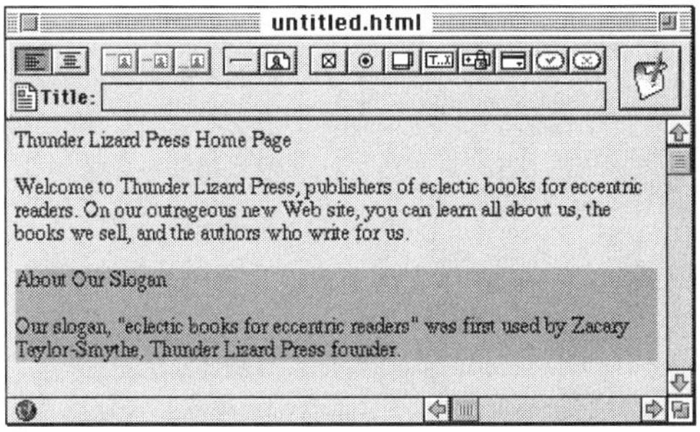

Figure 26. *To move text, begin by selecting it.*

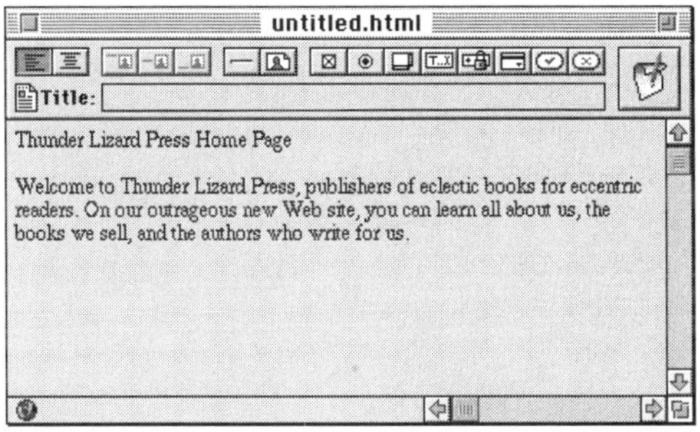

Figure 27. *When you use the Cut command, the text disappears.*

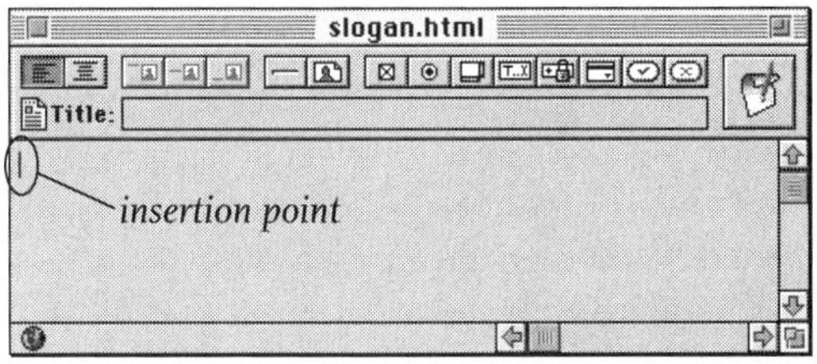

Figure 28. *Position the insertion point where you want the text to be moved. In this example, I've opened another PageMill document.*

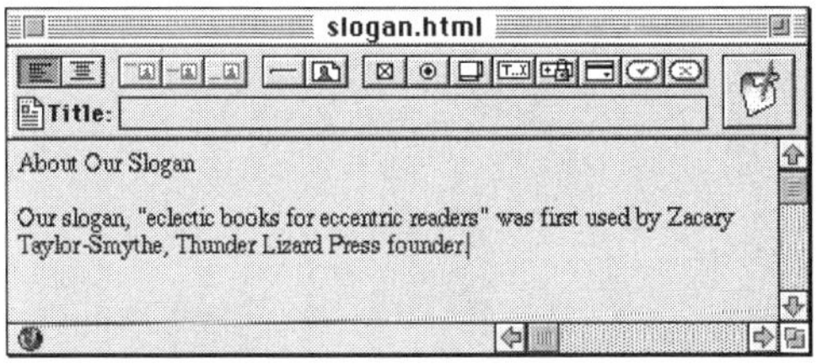

Figure 29. *When you use the Paste command, a copy of the Clipboard contents is pasted into the document.*

To move text with Cut & Paste

1. Select the text you want to move (see **Figure 26**).
2. Choose Cut from the Edit menu (see **Figure 20**).

   or

   Press [⌘X].

   The text is removed from the document and placed in the Clipboard (see **Figure 27**).
3. Position the insertion point where you want the cut text to be moved (see **Figure 28**).
4. Choose Paste from the Edit menu (see **Figure 20**).

   or

   Press [⌘V].

   A copy of the text in the Clipboard is pasted into the document at the insertion point (see **Figure 29**).

✔ Tips

- The Clipboard is a temporary holding place for information. Information is put on the Clipboard when you use the Copy or Cut command. It stays there until you use the Copy or Cut command again or shut off your Macintosh.
- You can use the Paste command to paste the contents of the Clipboard again and again in the same document or in other documents.
- You can use the Paste command to put a copy of the Clipboard contents into another PageMill document (see **Figures 28** and **29**) or any other document.
- You can also use Copy and Paste or Cut and Paste to take text from other documents and paste it into PageMill documents.

To move text with drag & drop

1. Select the text you want to move (see **Figure 30**).
2. Position the mouse pointer in the middle of the selected text. It turns into an arrow pointer (see **Figure 31**).
3. Press the mouse button down and drag. As you drag, a dotted line box the same size as the selection moves along with the mouse pointer. A blinking insertion point indicates where the text will go when you let go of the mouse button. You can see all this in **Figure 32**.
4. When the blinking insertion point is in the proper position, release the mouse button. The selected text moves (see **Figure 33**).

Figure 30. *Begin by selecting the text you want to move…*

Figure 31. *…then position the mouse pointer in the middle of the selection,…*

Figure 32. *…press the mouse button down, and drag to the new position.*

To copy text with drag & drop

1. Select the text you want to copy (see **Figure 30**).
2. Position the mouse pointer in the middle of the selected text. It turns into an arrow pointer (see **Figure 31**).
3. Hold down [Option] as you press the mouse button down and drag (see **Figure 32**).
4. When the blinking insertion point is in the proper position, release the mouse button. The selected text is copied (see **Figure 34**).

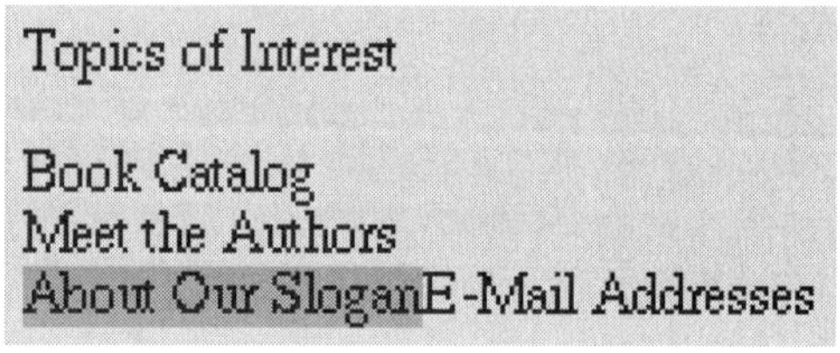

Figure 33. *When you release the mouse button, the selected text moves.*

✔ Tip

- You can drag and drop text to copy it from one document window to another —even between documents of different applications! It works with any application that supports Macintosh drag and drop, including SimpleText and the Scrapbook.

Figure 34. *If you press and hold* [Option] *while dragging, the selected text is copied rather than moved.*

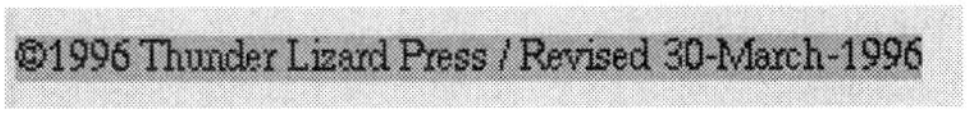

Figure 35. *Select the text you want to copy to the Pasteboard...*

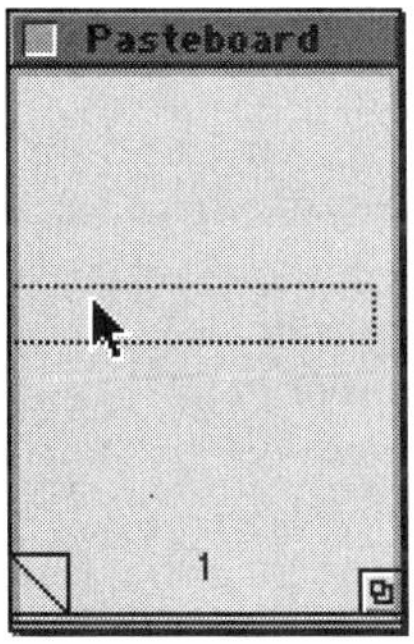

Figure 36. *...then drag it into the Pasteboard window.*

Figure 37. *Although text on the Pasteboard may look truncat-ed, it's all there.*

Figure 38. *Resizing the Pasteboard makes it easier to see its contents.*

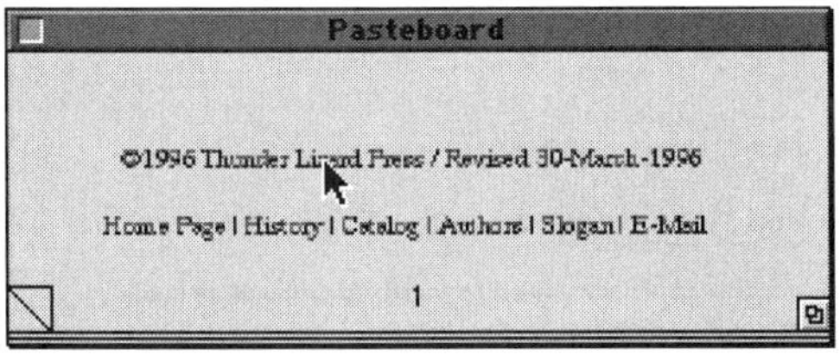

Figure 39. *To use an item in the Pasteboard, "grab it" with your mouse pointer and drag it into a PageMill document.*

To copy text to the Pasteboard

1. If the Pasteboard is not showing, choose Show Pasteboard from the Window menu or press ⌘/.
2. Select the text you want to put on the Pasteboard (see **Figure 35**).
3. Use the drag and drop techniques discussed on the previous page to drag the text from the PageMill document window to the Pasteboard window (see **Figure 36**).
4. When a selection border appears around the inside of the Pasteboard window (see **Figure 37**), release the mouse button. A copy of the selected text is placed on the Pasteboard (see **Figure 37**).

✔ Tips

- You can resize the Pasteboard by dragging its size box (see **Figure 38**).
- Although the Pasteboard has only five pages, you can copy more than one item to each page (see **Figure 39**).
- I tell you more about working with the Pasteboard in **Chapter 1**.

To use Pasteboard contents

1. Position the mouse pointer on the Pasteboard item you want to use (see **Figure 39**).
2. Use the drag and drop techniques discussed on the previous page to move (just drag) or copy (hold down Option while dragging) the item into position in a PageMill document.

✔ Tip

- Dragging an item off the Pasteboard is the only way to remove it from the Pasteboard.

About Undoing Actions

PageMill offers two commands to help you correct errors by undoing or reversing them:

- Undo reverses your last action.
- Revert to Saved throws away all changes you made to a document since the last time you saved it.

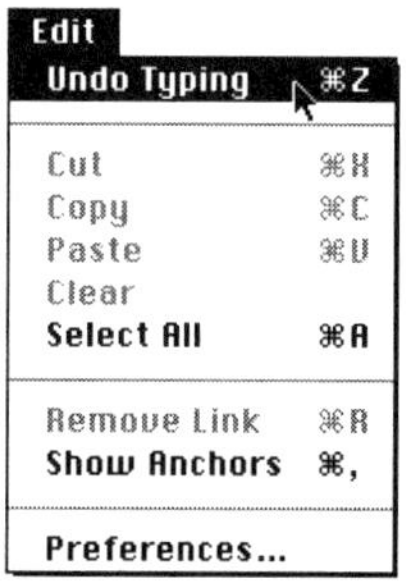

Figure 40. *The Undo command, which is the first one on the Edit menu, reverses your last action.*

To undo the last action

Choose Undo from the Edit menu.

or

Press ⌘Z.

The last action you performed is reversed.

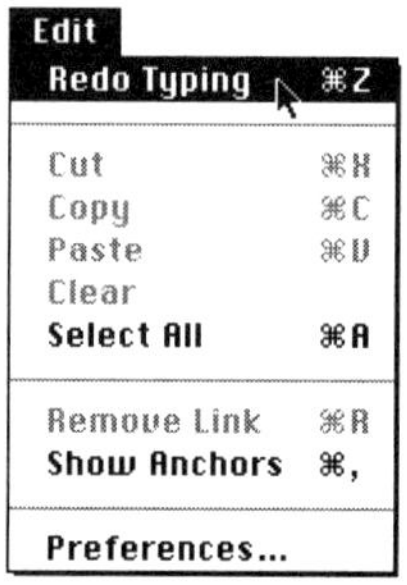

Figure 41. *If the last command you chose was Undo, the Undo command turns into the Redo command.*

✔ Tips

- The exact wording of this command depends on the last action you performed. For example, if the last thing you did was type text, the command will be Undo Typing (see **Figure 40**).
- If the Undo command is unavailable, the first command under the edit menu will be Cannot Undo, which will be gray.
- If the last action you performed was to use the Undo command, the first command under the Edit menu will be the Redo command (see **Figure 41**). This “undoes” the Undo command, restoring the document to the way it was before you chose Undo.

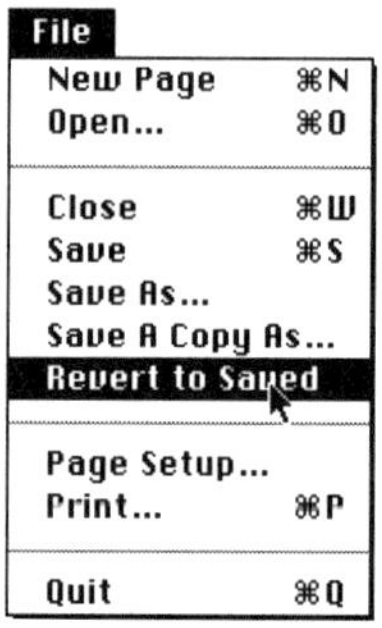

Figure 42. *Revert to Saved, throws out all the changes you made to a page since the last time you saved it.*

To revert to the saved page

1. Choose Revert to Saved from the File menu (see **Figure 42**).
2. A dialog box appears, asking you to confirm that you want to revert to the last saved version of the file (see **Figure 43**). Click Revert.

All changes you made to the file since the last time it was saved are reversed.

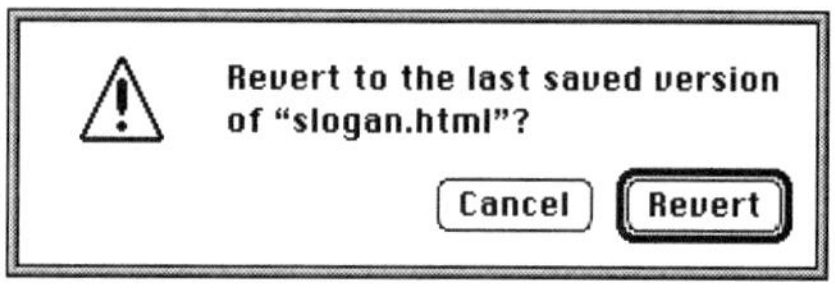

Figure 43. *When you choose the Revert to Saved command, PageMill asks if you really do want to revert to the last saved version of the file.*

About Saving Pages

When you save a page, you place a copy of it on disk. The finished version of the page will eventually wind up on your Web server, where other people on the Internet can access it.

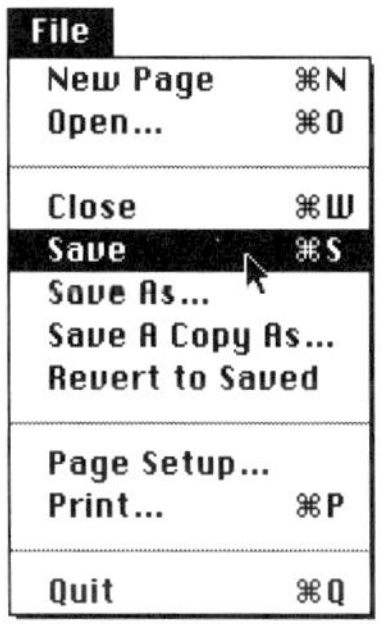

Figure 44. *PageMill offers three different commands to save a page file.*

✔ Tip

- Until you save a page file, it (or any change to it) exists only in your computer's random access memory (RAM). If your computer loses power or crashes, all work you've done since the last time you saved is lost. If you've never saved a page, the entire page is lost. This is why it's important to save frequently while you work.

To save a page for the first time

1. Choose Save (see **Figure 44**) or Save As from the File menu.

   or

   Press ⌘S.
2. Use the Save As dialog box that appears (see **Figure 45**) to open the folder in which you want to save the file.
3. Enter a name for the file in the Save File As edit box.
4. Click Save or press Return or Enter.

The file is saved in the folder you specified with the name you entered. The name you gave the file appears in the file's title bar (see **Figure 46**).

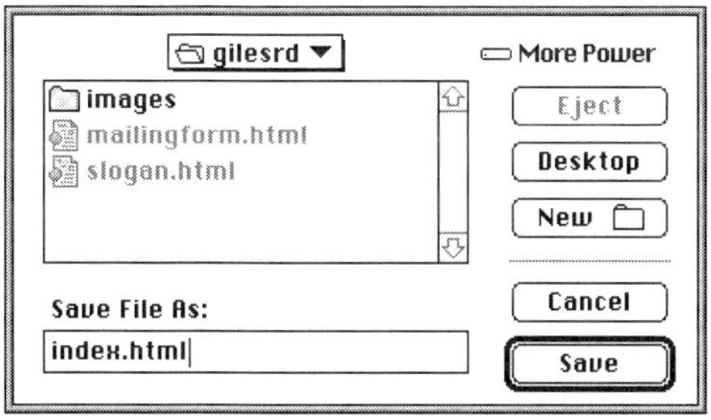

Figure 45. *Use the Save As dialog box to select a disk location and name a file. Click Save to complete the save.*

Figure 46. *The name of a saved page file appears in its title bar.*

✔ Tips

- The first time you save a file, both the Save and Save As commands do the same thing.
- Be sure to follow any file naming guidelines required by your server. If you're not sure what they are, ask the Webmaster or System Administrator.

To save changes to a saved page

Choose Save from the File menu (see **Figure 44**).

or

Press ⌘S.

If the page has already been saved, PageMill updates the file on disk to add your changes since the last save. It does not display any dialog box.

✔ Tip

- Save frequently as you work to prevent data loss in the event of a power outage or computer crash.

To save a page with a different name or in a different location

1. Choose Save As from the File menu (see **Figure 47**).
2. Use the Save As dialog box that appears to select a new folder and/or enter a new name.
3. Click Save or press Return or Enter.

The file is saved using the information you specified. If you changed the name of the file, its new name appears in the title bar. Subsequently using the Save command to save changes to the page will save changes to this new version, not the original.

To save a copy of a page

1. Choose Save A Copy As from the File menu (see **Figure 48**).
2. Use the Save As dialog box that appears (see **Figure 49**) to select a folder and/or enter a name for the copy.
3. Click Save or press Return or Enter.

The file is saved using the information you specified. Subsequently using the Save command to save changes to the page will save changes to the original version of the page, not the copy.

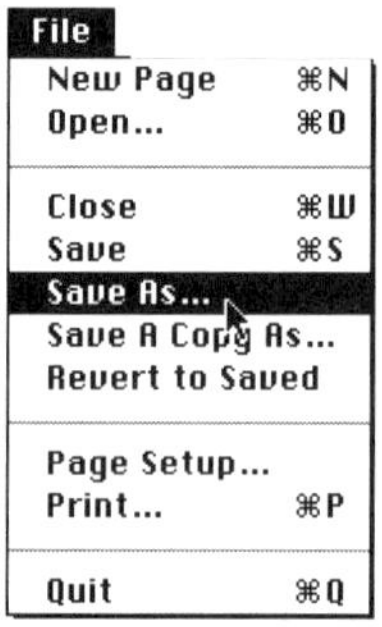

Figure 47. *Choose Save As from the File menu to save a page in a different folder or with a different name—or both.*

Figure 48. *The Save A Copy As command saves a copy of the current page.*

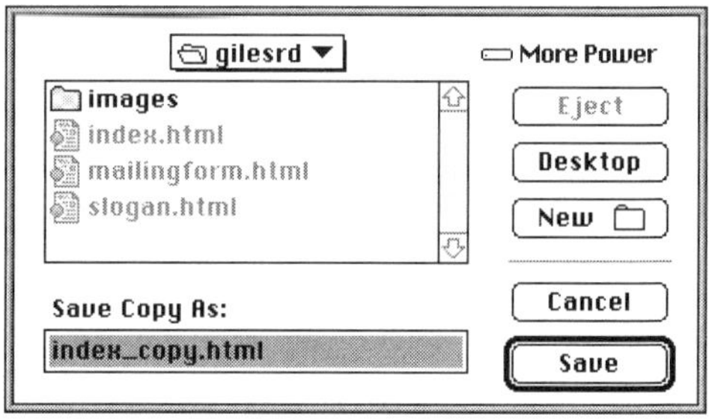

Figure 49. *You use the Save As dialog box to save a copy of a page, too.*

Saving Pages

About Printing

Even though Web pages are normally viewed on screen and are seldom printed, you can use the Page Setup and Print commands to prepare pages for printing and print them.

Figure 50. *Choose Page Setup from the File menu to specify page setup options before printing.*

To specify Page Setup options

1. Choose Page Setup from the File menu (see **Figure 50**).
2. In the Page Setup dialog box that appears (see **Figures 51a** and **51b** for examples), change settings for paper size, orientation, and other options as desired.
3. If the dialog box includes an Options button, click it to view and change other options if desired. When you're finished with that dialog box, click OK or press Return or Enter to save your settings.
4. Click OK or press Return or Enter in the Page Setup dialog box to save your settings.

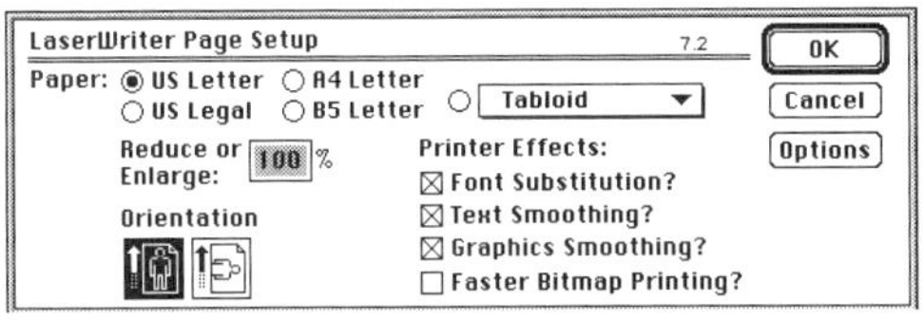

Figure 51a. *The appearance of the Page Setup dialog box varies depending on your selected printer driver. Here's what it looks like with a LaserWriter driver selected…*

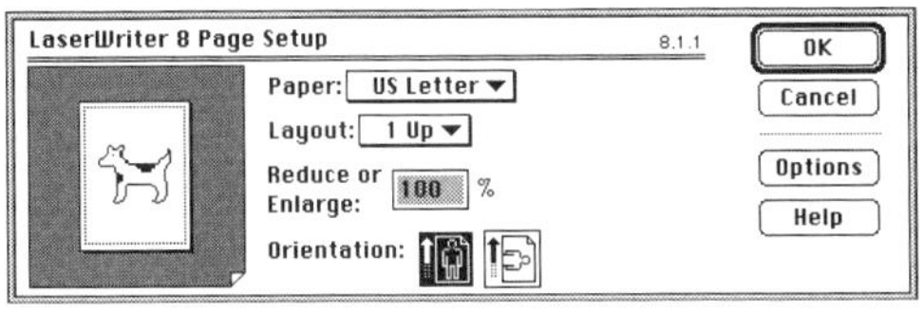

Figure 51b. *…and here's what it looks like with the LaserWriter 8 driver selected.*

✔ Tip

- The way the Page Setup dialog box appears (see **Figures 51a** and **51b** for examples) depends on your printer and the printer driver you selected in Apple's Chooser. Consult the documentation that came with your printer or Macintosh for more information about printer options or the Chooser.

To print a page

1. Choose Print from the File menu (see **Figure 52**).

   or

   Press ⌘ P.
2. In the Print dialog box that appears (see **Figures 53a** and **53b** for examples), set the number of copies, page range, and paper source.
3. To print the page's background (which I tell you about in **Chapter 7**), be sure to turn on the Print Background check box.
4. If the dialog box includes an Options button, click it to view and change other options if desired. When you're finished with that dialog box, click OK or press Return or Enter to save your settings.
5. Click Print or press Return or Enter to print.

Figure 52. *Choose Print from the File menu to print.*

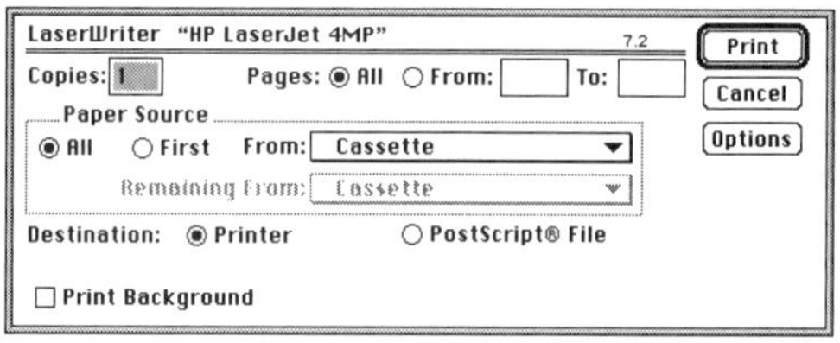

Figure 53a. *The selected printer driver also changes the way the Print dialog box looks. Here's a Print dialog box with the LaserWriter driver selected…*

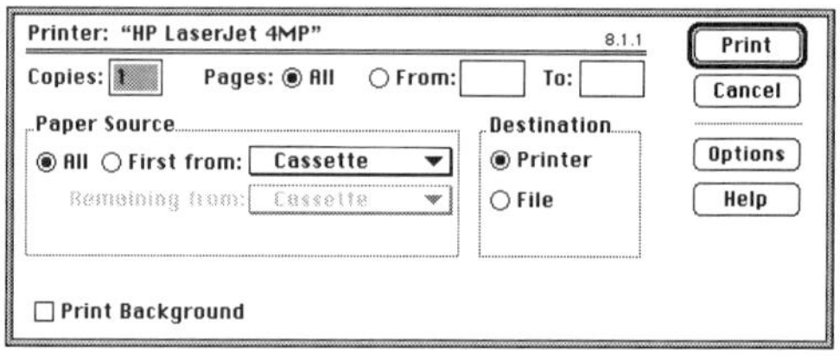

Figure 53b. *…and here's the same dialog box with the LaserWriter 8 driver selected. Can you see the subtle differences?*

✔ Tips

- The way the Print dialog box appears depends on your printer and the printer driver you selected in Apple's Chooser. Consult the documentation that came with your printer or Macintosh for more information about printer options or the Chooser.
- PageMill automatically paginates documents when it prints them. You cannot override its page breaks. It will not, however, break a page in the middle of a graphic object.

About Windows

Like most other Macintosh applications, PageMill enables you to have more than one document window open at a time.

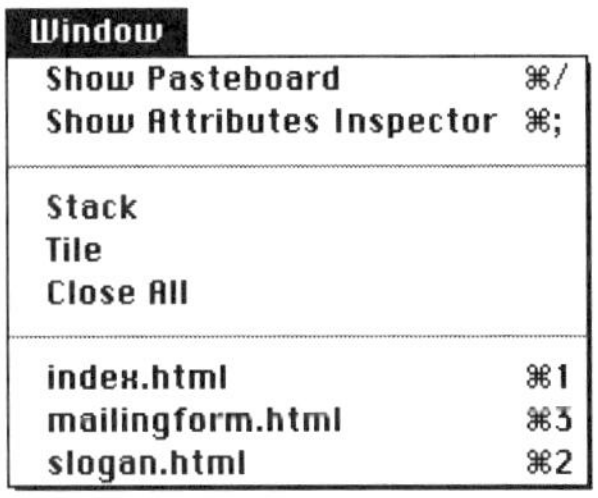

Figure 54. *The Window menu offers commands for working with windows.*

✔ Tips

- The active window is the one with the striped title bar.
- You can resize a window by clicking its zoom box or dragging its size box.
- You can move a window by dragging its title bar.

To switch windows

Click any exposed portion of the window with which you want to work.

or

Choose the name of the window with which you want to work from the Window menu (see **Figure 54**).

The window you clicked or chose comes to the front and becomes the active window.

Figure 55. *Stacking windows shows the title bar for each window, without resizing any of them.*

✔ Tip

- Each window has a Command key equivalent consisting of [⌘] and a number (see **Figure 54**). You can press a window's key combination to switch to that window.

To arrange windows

- To stack windows, choose Stack from the Window menu (see **Figure 54**). The windows are neatly stacked, without being resized, with the active window on top (see **Figure 55**).
- To tile windows, choose Tile from the Window menu (see **Figure 54**). The windows are resized and tiled across the entire screen (see **Figure 56**), with the active window on top.

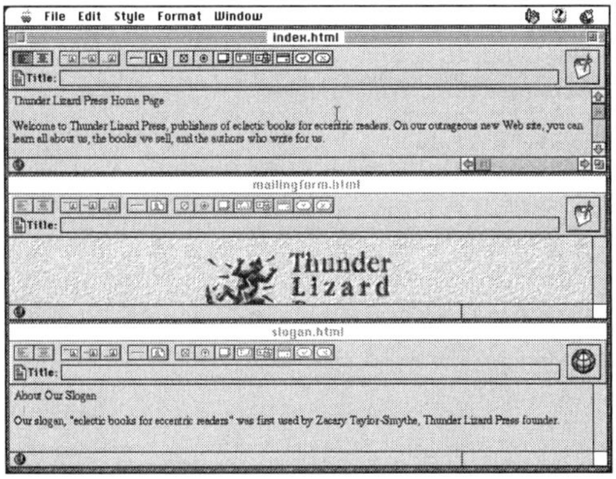

Figure 56. *Tiling windows resizes them so they fill the screen.*

To close a window

1. If necessary, switch to the window you want to close.
2. Choose Close from the File menu (see **Figure 57**).

   or

   Press [⌘][W].

   or

   Click the window's close box.
3. If you have made changes to the contents of the window since the last time you saved it, a dialog box like the one in **Figure 58** appears.
   - ▲ Click Save or press [Return] or [Enter] to save the changes. If you have never saved the file at all, a Save As dialog box appears so you can choose a folder, enter a name, and save the file.
   - ▲ Click Don't Save to close the window without saving changes.
   - ▲ Click Cancel to dismiss the dialog box without closing the window.

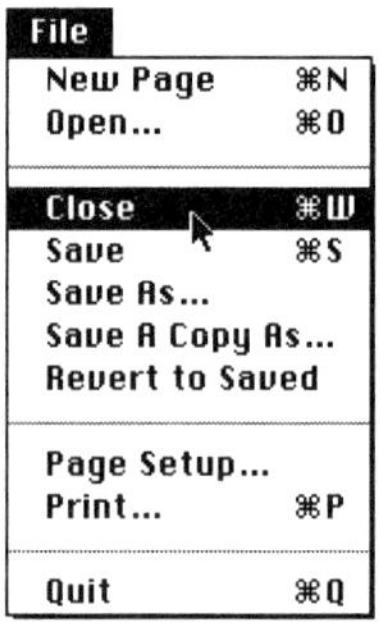

Figure 57. *Choose Close from the File menu to close the active window.*

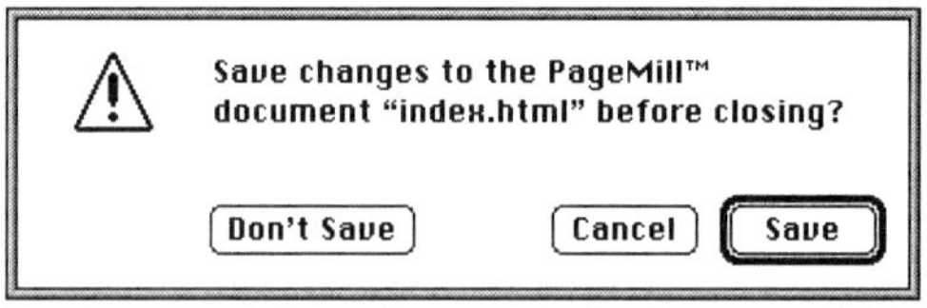

Figure 58. *If you try to close a window with unsaved changes, a dialog box like this one appears.*

To close all windows

Choose Close All from the Window menu (see **Figure 59**).

A dialog box like the one in **Figure 58** appears for every window whose contents you have changed since you last saved it. Follow the instructions in step 3 above to dismiss this dialog box each time it appears.

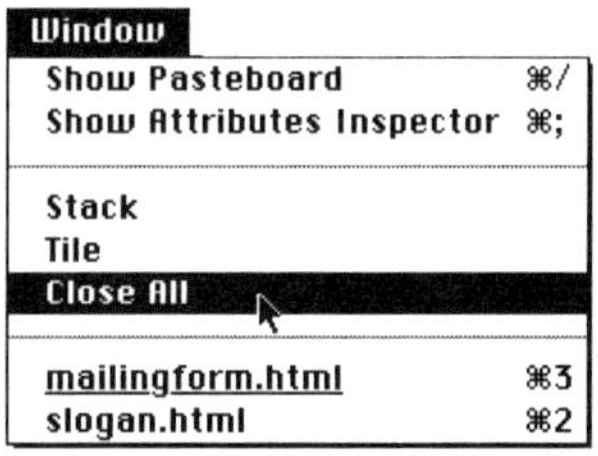

Figure 59. *To close all windows at once, choose Close All from the Window menu.*

APPLYING CHARACTER STYLES 3

About Character Styles

In HTML, the underlying language of the World Wide Web, there are two kinds of text formatting:

- *Physical Styles* use tags to specify how text should look, regardless of its use within the document. A physical style like bold, for example, will always look bold, no matter how it is used in the document or which Web browser is used to view it.
- *Logical Styles* use tags to specify how text should look based on its use within a document. A logical style like strong, for example, may appear bold when viewed with some browsers and underlined when viewed with others. The point is, strong-formatted characters are formatted differently from unformatted characters, making them stand out.

The main problem with using logical styles is that you can't always predict how logical style-formatted characters will appear when viewed with various Web browsers. For that reason, you may prefer to use physical styles.

Of course, no matter what kind of character formatting you apply, PageMill takes care of inserting the proper tags for you. You simply select the text you want to format and choose the style you want from the Style menu or press the appropriate Command key equivalent.

✔ Tip

- Formatting individual text characters is occasionally referred to as *highlighting* since formatted characters stand out from unformatted characters.

About Physical Styles

PageMill supports four physical styles:

- *Plain* is plain text, without formatting.
- *Bold* is bold text.
- *Italic* is italicized text.
- *Teletype* is monospaced text.

Figure 1 shows an example of each of these physical styles.

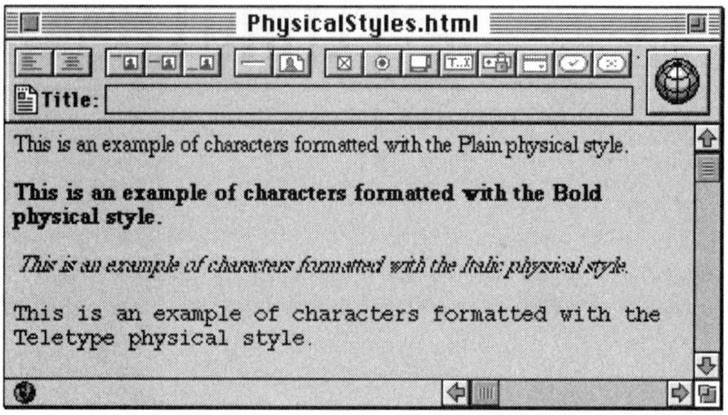

Figure 1. *PageMill's four physical styles.*

To apply a physical style

1. Select the text you want to format (see **Figure 2**).
2. Choose one of the following commands from the Style menu (see **Figure 3**):
   - ▲ For plain text, choose Plain.
   - ▲ For bold style, choose Bold.
   - ▲ For italic style, choose Italic.
   - ▲ For monospaced type, choose Teletype.

   or

   Press one of the following Command key equivalents:
   - ▲ For plain text, press Shift ⌘ P.
   - ▲ For bold style, press ⌘ B.
   - ▲ For italic style, press ⌘ I.
   - ▲ For monospaced type, press Shift ⌘ T.

The selected text changes to the style you specified (see **Figure 4**).

Figure 2. *Begin by selecting the text you want to format…*

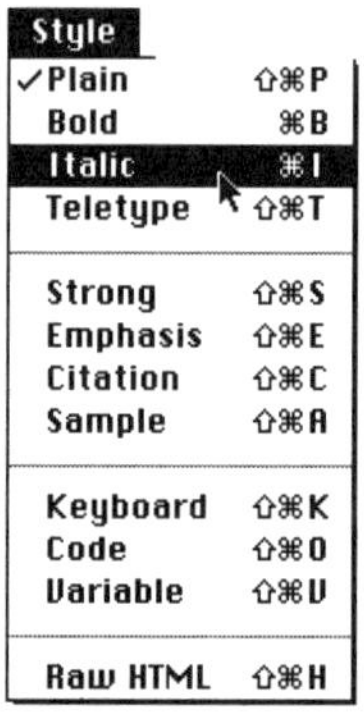

Figure 3. *…then choose the physical style you want to apply from the Style menu.*

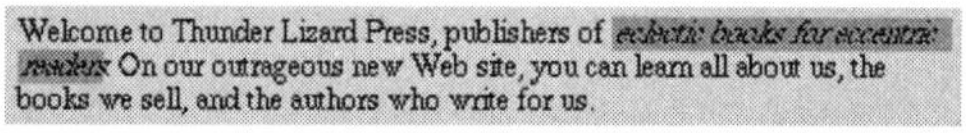

Figure 4. *The style you chose — in this case Italic — is applied immediately.*

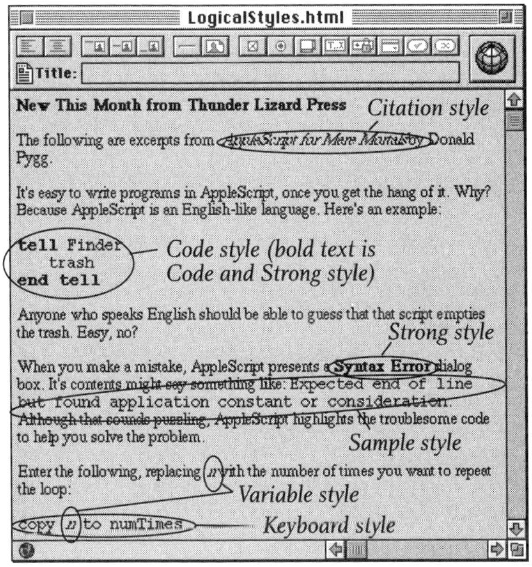

Figure 5. *Six of PageMill's seven logical styles in action.*

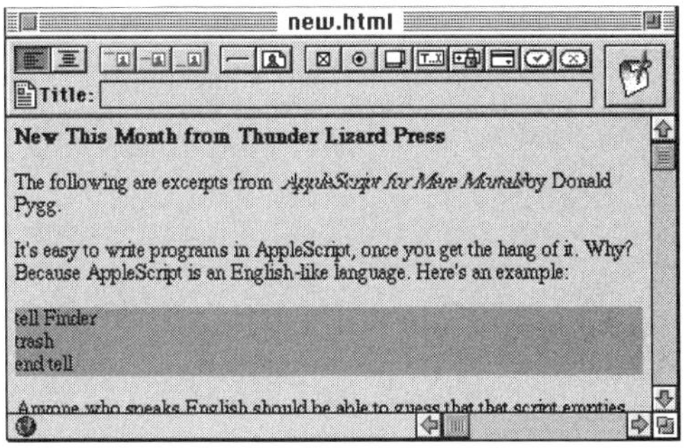

Figure 6. *Select the text you want to format.*

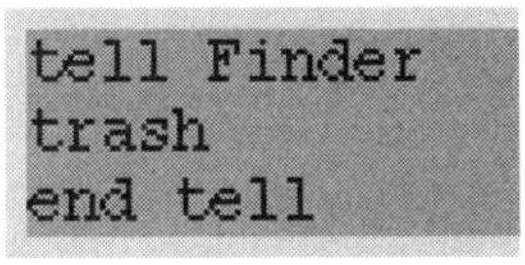

Figure 7. *The selected text changes to the style you apply.*

About Logical Styles

PageMill supports seven logical styles:

- *Strong* is for strong emphasis.
- *Emphasis* is for emphasis.
- *Citation* is for the titles of books and other references.
- *Sample* is for computer status messages.
- *Keyboard* is for user keyboard entry.
- *Code* is for computer programming code.
- *Variable* is for variables which must be replaced by the user.

Figure 5 shows an example of how logical styles can be used. Remember, the appearance of logical styles may vary from one Web browser to another.

To apply a logical style

1. Select the text you want to format (see **Figure 6**).
2. Choose one of the logical styles—Strong, Emphasis, Citation, Sample, Keyboard, Code, or Variable—from the Style menu (see **Figure 3**).

   or

   Press one of the following Command key equivalents:

   - For Strong style, press Shift ⌘ S.
   - For Emphasis style, press Shift ⌘ E.
   - For Citation style, press Shift ⌘ C.
   - For Sample style, press Shift ⌘ A.
   - For Keyboard style, press Shift ⌘ K.
   - For Code style, press Shift ⌘ O.
   - For Variable style, press Shift ⌘ V.

The selected text changes to the style you specified (see **Figure 7**).

✔ Tips

- You can apply more than one style to text. Simply select each style, one at a time, from the Style menu while the text is selected. **Figure 8** shows an example of text with bold and italic style applied.
- You can combine physical and logical styles if desired. For example, you can apply Bold and Emphasis styles to get bold, italic-looking text. Just remember that the appearance of logical styles varies from one Web browser to another, so you may not get the results you expect on all browsers.
- If you're not sure what style is applied to characters, select them and pull down the Style menu. As illustrated in **Figures 3**, **9**, and **11**, a check mark appears beside the name of each style applied to selected text. (This technique does not work when different styles are applied to characters within a selection.)
- You can apply character styles to text already formatted with paragraph formatting. I tell you about paragraph formatting in **Chapter 4**.
- Character styles do not change the way PageMill or Web browsers treat multiple spaces, tabs, or returns in a page document. These characters are stripped out as discussed in **Chapter 2**. In order to include additional spaces or empty lines, use Preformatted paragraph formatting. I discuss paragraph formatting in **Chapter 4**.
- Although Raw HTML is included on the Style menu, it does not change the appearance of selected text. Instead, it enables you to manually enter HTML tags in your PageMill pages. I tell you how to use the Raw HTML command in **Chapter 9**.

Figure 8. *You can apply more than one style to selected text.*

Style Application Tips

About Removing Styles

When you apply a style you, in effect, "turn it on" for selected text. To remove a style, simply "turn it off."

To remove a style

1. Select the text from which you want to remove the style (see **Figure 8**).
2. Choose the name of the style you want to remove from the Style menu (see **Figure 9**).

   or

   Press the Command key equivalent for the style you want to remove.

The style you chose is removed from the selected text (see **Figure 10**).

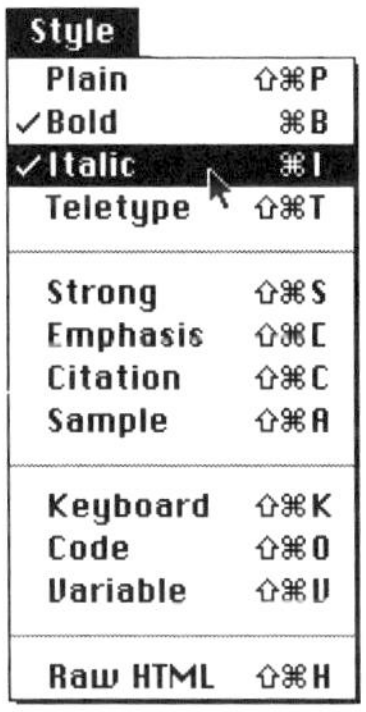

Figure 9. *To remove an applied style, simply choose it from the Style menu.*

Figure 10. *By removing or "turning off" the Italic style, the text in* Figure 8 *retains only its Bold style.*

To remove all styles

1. Select the text from which you want to remove all styles (see **Figure 8**).
2. Choose Plain from the Style menu (see **Figure 11**).

   or

   Press [Shift][⌘][P].

All styles are removed from the selected text.

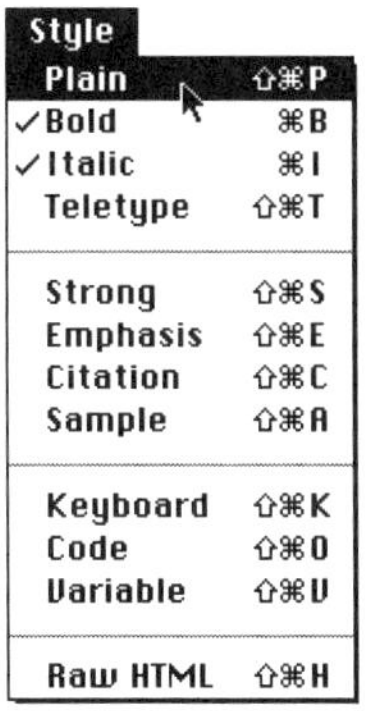

Figure 11. *To remove all styles, choose Plain from the Style menu.*

✔ Tip

- If the above techniques do not remove a physical style, some kind of paragraph formatting is probably applied to the text. You must remove the paragraph formatting to change the appearance of the text. I tell you about paragraph formatting in **Chapter 4**.

About the Attributes Inspector's Character Style Options

The Attributes Inspector offers another way to apply and remove character styles. Rather than use menu commands or Command key equivalents, simply select text and turn Attributes Inspector check boxes on or off.

To apply styles with the Attributes Inspector

1. If the Attributes Inspector is not displayed, choose Show Attributes Inspector from the Window menu (see **Figure 12**) or press ⌘ ;.
2. If necessary, click the Text button on the Attributes Inspector's button bar (see **Figure 13**) to display the Text options.
3. In the page document window, select the text to which you want to apply a style.
4. In the Attributes Inspector, turn on the check box corresponding to the style you want to apply.
5. Repeat steps 3 and 4 to apply styles throughout the document.

Figure 12. *Choose Show Attributes Inspector from the Window menu.*

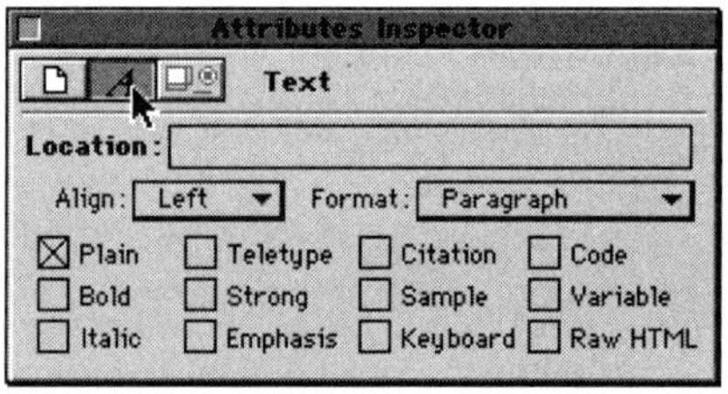

Figure 13. *When you click the Text button on the Attributes Inspector's button bar, you get access to text formatting options.*

To remove styles with the Attributes Inspector

1. Follow Steps 1 and 2 above, if necessary, to display the Attributes Inspector and its Text options.
2. In the page document window, select the text from which you want to remove styles.
3. In the Attributes Inspector, turn off the check box corresponding to the style you want to remove.

   or

   Turn on the Plain check box to remove all character styles.

✔ Tips

- The concepts presented throughout this chapter also apply when using the Attributes Inspector to apply or remove styles.
- The Text options of the Attributes Inspector also enable you to apply paragraph formatting. I tell you about paragraph formatting in **Chapter 4**.

APPLYING PARAGRAPH FORMATS 4

About Paragraph Formats

Unlike character styles, which I discuss in **Chapter 3**, paragraph formats are used to format entire paragraphs of information.

PageMill supports a wide range of HTML paragraph formatting options:

- *Alignment* options specify the way text is positioned between the left and right sides of the window.
- *Indentation* options specify the amount of space between the left side of the window and the text.
- *Heading* options specify the size of headings.
- *List* options specify the way lists of information appear.
- *Preformatted* formatting enables you to create tables of information.
- *Address* formatting applies special formatting to addresses.

No matter what kind of paragraph formatting you apply, PageMill takes care of inserting HTML tags for you. You simply select the paragraph(s) you want to format, then choose the format option you want.

✔ Tips

- In PageMill (as in most other programs), a paragraph is defined by return characters. Each time you press Return, you end the current paragraph and begin a new one.
- When applying paragraph formatting to only one paragraph, just position the insertion point in the paragraph before choosing the formatting option. Formatting is applied to the entire paragraph.

About Alignment

PageMill's alignment options specify the way text is positioned between the left and right sides of the browser window. PageMill offers two options:

- *Left Align* aligns text with the left side of the window.
- *Center Align* centers text between the left and right sides of the window.

Figure 1 shows an example of each alignment option.

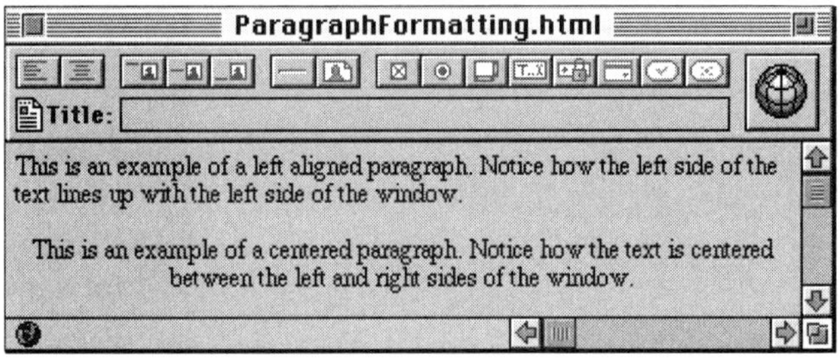

Figure 1. *PageMill's text alignment options.*

✔ Tip

- By default, text is left aligned.

To set paragraph alignment

1. Select all or part of the paragraph(s) whose alignment you want to change (see **Figure 2**).
2. Click the alignment button corresponding to the alignment option you want (see **Figure 3**).

   or

   Press ⌘ Control ← to left align the paragraph.

   or

   Press ⌘ Control → to center align the paragraph.

The selected paragraph(s) change accordingly (see **Figure 4**).

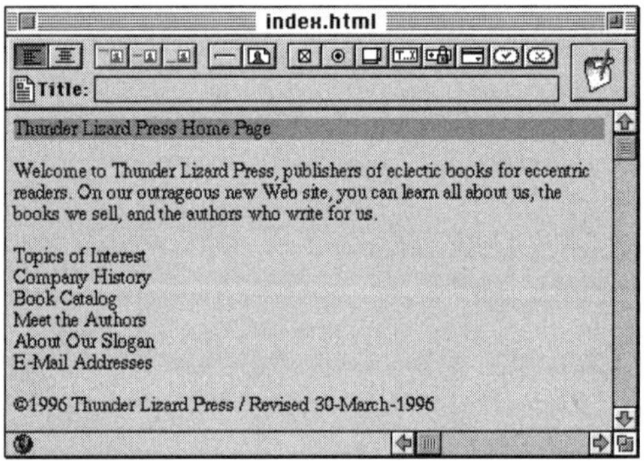

Figure 2. *Select the paragraph(s) you want to format.*

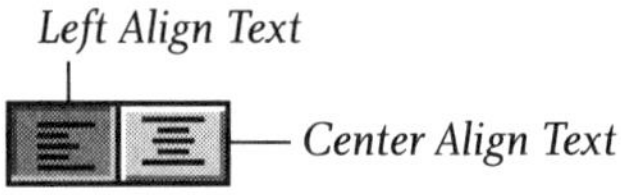

Figure 3. *Use one of the text alignment buttons on the button bar to set alignment for selected paragraph(s).*

Figure 4. *Here's the selection from* Figure 2 *after clicking the Center Align Text button.*

About Indentation

PageMill's indentation options specify the amount of space between the left side of the browser window and the text.

- *Indent Left* removes space between the text and the left side of the window.
- *Indent Right* adds space between the text and the left side of the window.

Figure 5 shows an example of each indentation option.

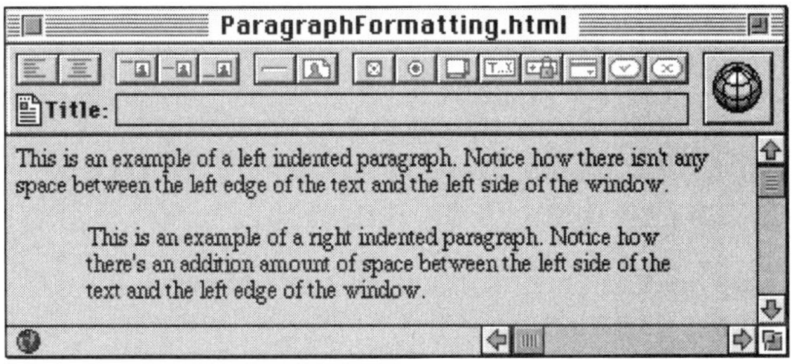

Figure 5. *PageMill's text indentation options.*

✔ Tip

- By default, text is left indented.

To set paragraph indentation

1. Select all or part of the paragraph(s) whose indentation you want to change (see **Figure 6**).
2. Choose the indentation option you want—Indent Left or Indent Right—from the Format menu (see **Figure 7**).

   or

   Press ⌘[to left indent the paragraph.

   or

   Press ⌘] to right indent the paragraph.

The selected paragraph(s) change accordingly (see **Figure 8**).

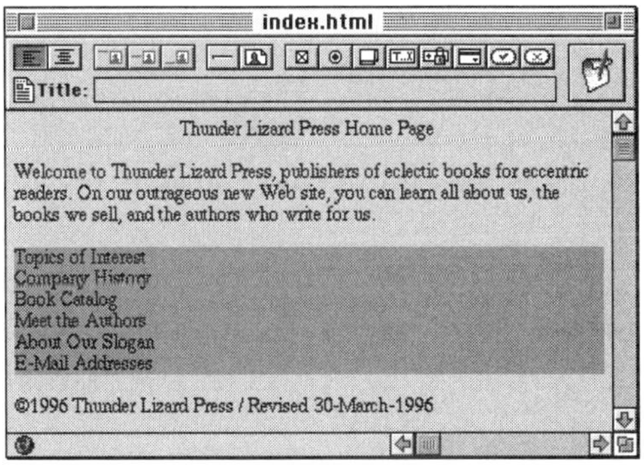

Figure 6. *Select the paragraph(s) you want to format.*

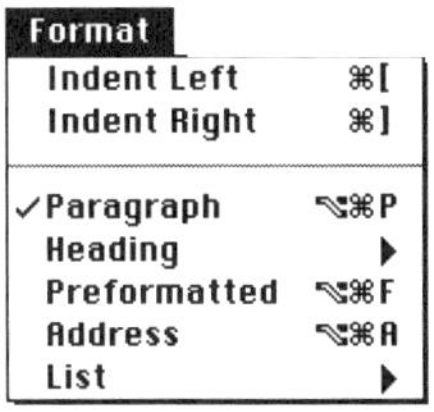

Figure 7. *Choose the indentation option you want from the Format menu.*

Figure 8. *Here's the selection from* Figure 6 *after choosing Indent Right from the Format menu.*

About Headings

PageMill's heading options let you choose from among six heading levels, each of which applies a different text size:

- *Large, Larger,* and *Largest* set headings larger than the standard text size.
- *Small, Smaller,* and *Smallest* set headings at the same size or smaller than the standard text size.

Paragraphs formatted as headings also have bold style applied and blank lines added before and after them. **Figure 9** illustrates each heading option. You can see the line spacing changes more clearly in **Figures 12** and **13**.

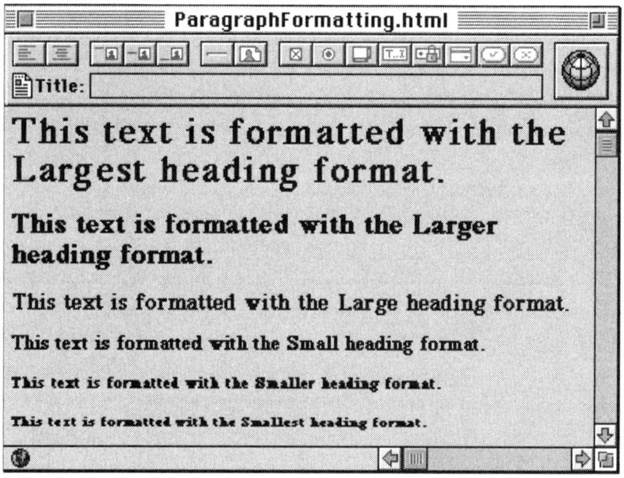

Figure 9. *PageMill's heading formats.*

✔ Tips

- By default, no heading is applied.
- Heading formats offer the only way to change font size within PageMill.

To apply a heading format

1. Select all or part of the paragraph(s) you want to format as a heading (see **Figure 10**).
2. Choose the heading option you want from the Heading submenu under the Format menu (see **Figure 11**).

   or

   Press Option ⌘ 1 through Option ⌘ 3 for Largest, Larger, and Large headings.

   or

   Press Option ⌘ 4 through Option ⌘ 6 for Small, Smaller, and Smallest headings.

The selected paragraph(s) change accordingly (see **Figure 12**).

Figure 10. *Select the paragraph(s) you want to format as headings.*

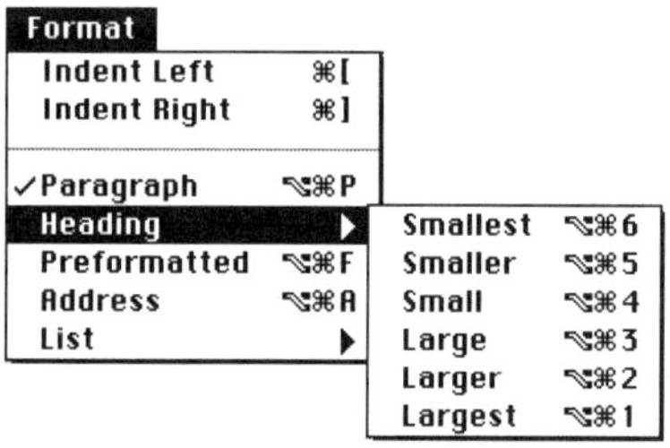

Figure 11. *Choose a heading option from the Heading submenu under the Format menu.*

Figure 12. *Here's the paragraph selected in* Figure 10 *with the Larger heading applied, as well as another paragraph with the Large heading applied. Note the blank line added after each of the headings.*

Figure 13. *This example has several headings, some of which have additional formatting or styles applied.*

Figure 14. *Choose Paragraph from the Format menu to remove heading formats from selected paragraphs.*

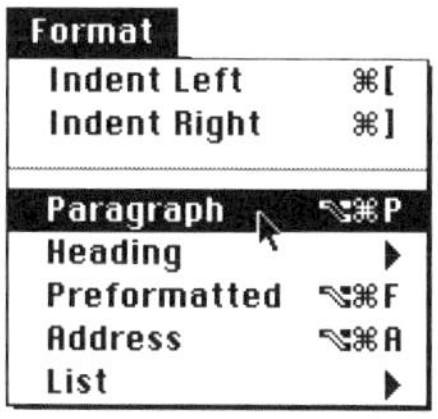

✔ Tips

- The Command key equivalents for the heading formats correspond to the HTML tags. For example, the HTML tag for the largest heading format is <H1>; the Command key equivalent for the same heading format in PageMill is Option ⌘ 1. This makes it easy for PageMill users with HTML knowledge to remember the Command key equivalents.
- You can see which heading format is applied to a paragraph by selecting the paragraph and looking at the Heading submenu under the Format menu. A check mark appears beside the format that is applied. (This technique may not work if you select multiple paragraphs with different formatting applied.)
- You can combine heading formats with other formatting and style options to achieve the effects you want. **Figure 13** shows an example of two centered headings, one of which has Italic style applied. I discuss character styles in **Chapter 3**.
- You cannot remove the Bold style from a heading. I discuss character styles in **Chapter 3**.

To remove a heading format

1. Select the paragraph(s) with the heading format applied.
2. Choose Paragraph from the Format menu (see **Figure 14**).

   or

   Press Option ⌘ P.

The heading format is removed.

About List Formats

PageMill's six list format options let you create a variety of nicely formatted lists:

- *Bullet* creates a bulleted list. The bullets are inserted automatically.
- *Directory* creates a bulleted list. The bullets are inserted automatically.
- *Menu* creates an indented list.
- *Numbered* creates a numbered list. The numbers are inserted automatically.
- *Definition* indents the paragraph. It is designed to be used with Term.
- *Term*, when used with Definition, lets you create glossary-style lists.

Figure 15 illustrates the list formats. (Directory format, which is not illustrated, is identical in appearance to Bullet format.)

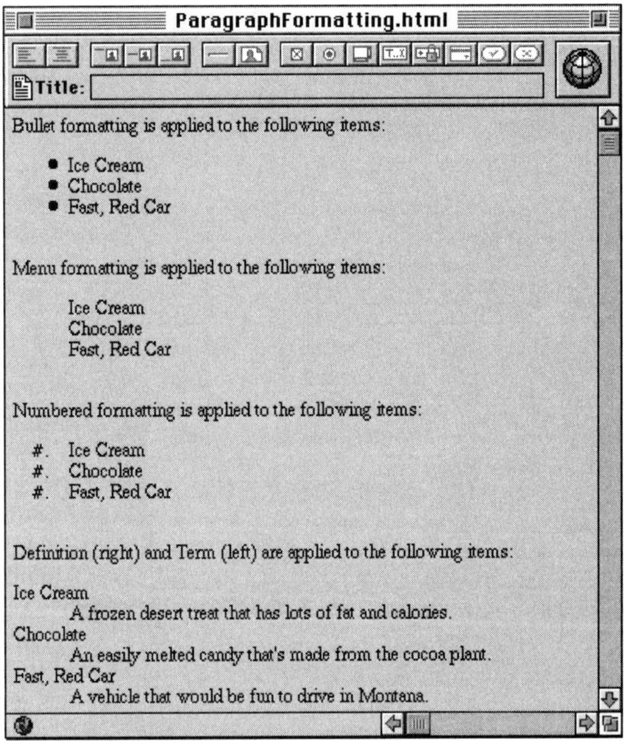

Figure 15. *PageMill's list formats.*

✔ Tips

- By default, no list formatting is applied.
- Paragraphs formatted as a list also have a blank line inserted above and below them.
- When you create a numbered list, PageMill displays pound signs (#) where the numbers should go (see **Figure 15**). Don't worry—when your page is viewed with a Web browser, the numbers will appear.

Figure 16. *Select the paragraphs you want to include in the list.*

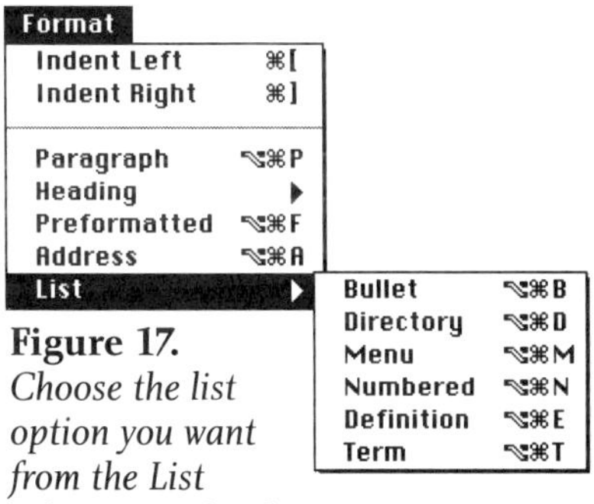

Figure 17. *Choose the list option you want from the List submenu under the Format menu.*

Figure 18. *Here's the selection from* Figure 16 *formatted as a bulleted list.*

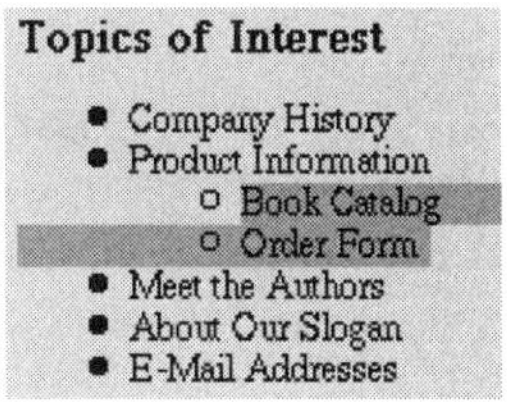

Figure 19. *To create a nested list, select the items you want to indent and choose Indent Right from the Format menu.*

To create a list

1. Select all or part of the paragraphs you want to include in your list (see **Figure 16**).
2. Choose the list option you want—Bullet, Directory, Menu, Numbered, Definition, or Term—from the List submenu under the Format menu (see **Figure 17**).

   or

   Press the Command key equivalent for the list option you want:

   - For Bullet, press Option ⌘ B.
   - For Directory, press Option ⌘ D.
   - For Menu, press Option ⌘ M.
   - For Numbered, press Option ⌘ N.
   - For Definition, press Option ⌘ E.
   - For Term, press Option ⌘ T.

The selected paragraphs change to become part of a list (see **Figure 18**).

✔ Tip

- To create a nested list, select the list items you want to indent and choose Indent Right from the Format menu or press ⌘]. The items are indented and the bullet or numbering scheme changes (see **Figure 19**).

To remove list formats

1. Select the paragraph(s) from which you want to remove the list format.
2. Choose Paragraph from the Format menu (see **Figure 14**).

   or

   Press Option ⌘ P.

The list format is removed from the selection.

To create a definition list

1. Enter the text for the list by alternating between terms and definitions (see **Figure 20**).
2. Select a term in the list (see **Figure 21**).
3. Choose Term from the List submenu under the Format menu (see **Figure 17**).

   or

   Press Option ⌘ T.

   A blank line appears beneath the term (see **Figure 22**).
4. Select the definition immediately following the term you just formatted (see **Figure 23**).
5. Choose Definition from the List submenu under the Format menu (see **Figure 17**).

   or

   Press Option ⌘ E.

   The definition moves up under the term and blank line appears below it (see **Figure 24**).
6. Repeat steps 2 through 5 for each term and definition in the list.

When you're finished, your list might look something like the one in **Figure 25**.

-I-

In Print
A book that is still in production. Opposite: out of print.
Index
A listing of key terms used throughout a book with corresponding page reference numbers. An index is usually at the end of a book.
ISBN
A reference number for a book consisting of a publisher-specific prefix and additional unique digits.

Figure 20. *Begin by entering the terms and definitions you want to include in the definition list.*

In Print
A book that is still in production. Opposite: out of print.

Figure 21. *Select a term in the list.*

In Print

A book that is still in production. Opposite: out of print.

Figure 22. *When you apply Term formatting, a blank line appears beneath the term.*

In Print

A book that is still in production. Opposite: out of print.

Figure 23. *Select the definition beneath the formatted term.*

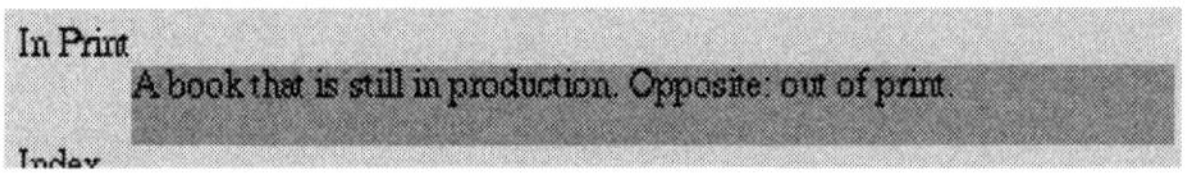
In Print
A book that is still in production. Opposite: out of print.

Figure 24. *When you apply Definition formatting, the definition moves up and becomes indented.*

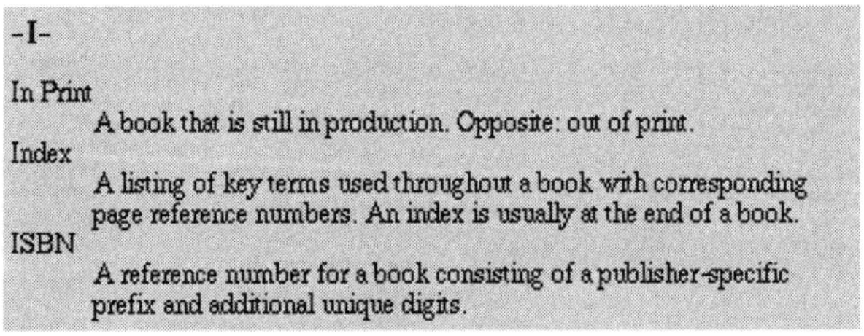
-I-

In Print
A book that is still in production. Opposite: out of print.
Index
A listing of key terms used throughout a book with corresponding page reference numbers. An index is usually at the end of a book.
ISBN
A reference number for a book consisting of a publisher-specific prefix and additional unique digits.

Figure 25. *A completed definition list.*

✔ Tip

- A quicker way to format the list may be to format all paragraphs in the list (terms and definitions) with Term format and then reformat the definition paragraphs with Definition format.

Figure 26a. *A table created with extra space characters in PageMill…*

Figure 26b. *…will look like this when viewed with a Web browser like Netscape Navigator.*

About Preformatted Paragraphs

Normally extra space and return characters in HTML documents are ignored by Web browsers. So although you might work hard to create a table like the one in **Figure 26a**, when it's viewed by a Web browser, the page will look like the one in **Figure 26b**.

Preformatted formatting solves this problem. It combines a monospaced font with the ability to include as many extra space and return characters as you like. This makes it possible to create formatted tables like the one in **Figures 27a** and **27b**.

✔ Tips

- While creating a table like the one in **Figure 26a**, PageMill leads you to believe that the spaces will remain between columns by displaying the page the same way in both Page and Preview modes. But if you save and close the page, then reopen it, PageMill's Page and Preview modes show a more realistic view of the page, more in line with **Figure 26b**.
- Using a monospaced style like Code or Sample is not the same as using the Preformatted format. Styles will not retain the extra spaces. I tell you about styles in **Chapter 3**.

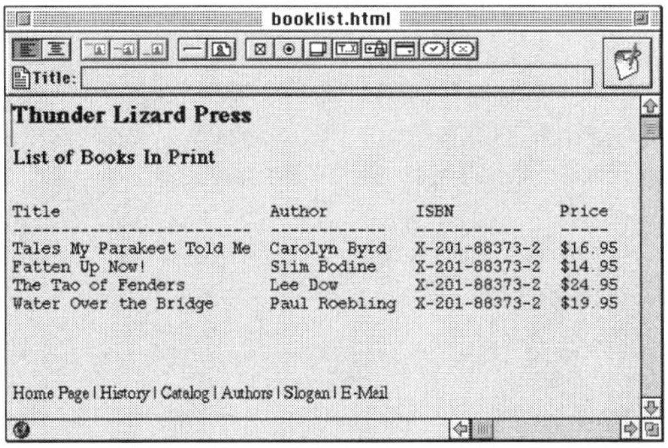

Figure 27a. *But if you use Preformatted format, the spaces remain…*

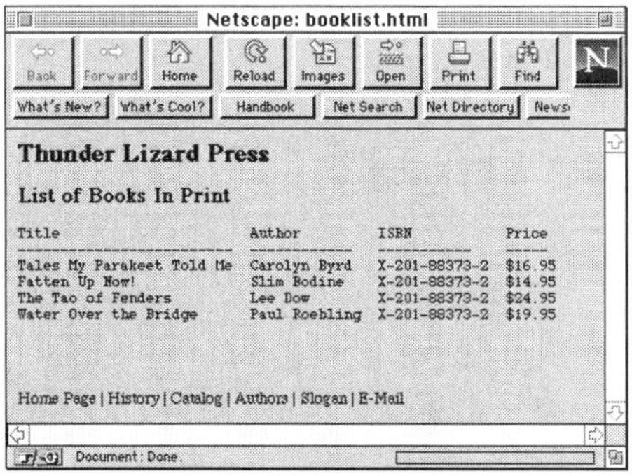

Figure 27b. *…so the page looks like this when viewed with a Web browser.*

To apply the Preformatted format to existing text

1. Select all or part of the paragraph(s) to which you want to apply the Preformatted format (see **Figure 28**).
2. Choose Preformatted from the Format menu (see **Figure 7**).

   or

   Press [Option][⌘][F].

The selected paragraph(s) change accordingly (see **Figure 29**). You can then add spaces, if necessary, to get the desired formatting effect (see **Figure 30**).

Figure 28. *Select the paragraph(s) to which you want to apply Preformatted format.*

To use the Preformatted format as you enter text

1. Position the insertion point on an empty line where you want the preformatted text to begin (see **Figure 31**).
2. Choose Preformatted from the Format menu (see **Figure 7**).

   or

   Press [Option][⌘][F].

   This "turns on" preformatted formatting.
3. Type the text you want preformatted. It is entered in monospaced type (see **Figure 32**).
4. Press [Return] after the last line of preformatted text (see **Figure 33**).
5. Choose Paragraph from the Format menu (see **Figure 14**).

   or

   Press [Option][⌘][P].

   This "turns off" preformatted formatting.

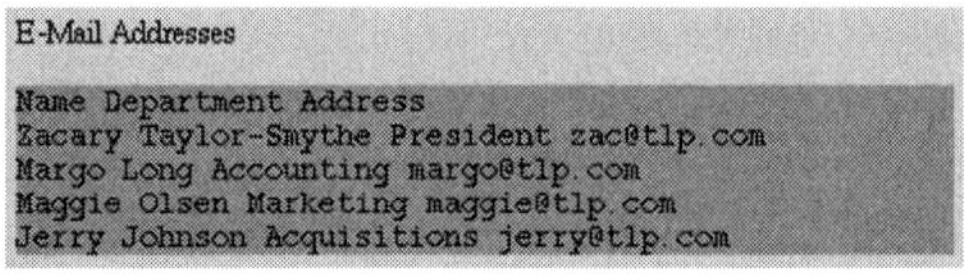

Figure 29. *When you apply the Preformatted format, the text changes.*

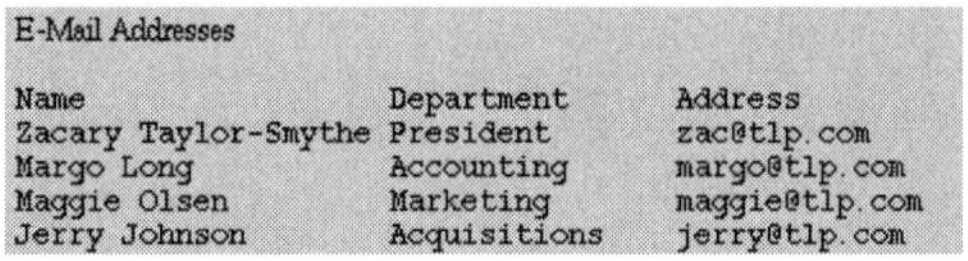

Figure 30. *Here's the table from* Figures 28 *and* 29 *with additional spaces added.*

Figure 31. *Position the insertion point where you want to begin preformatted text.*

Figure 32. *As you type, text is entered in monospaced type.*

Figure 33. *Press* [Return] *after the last line of preformatted text.*

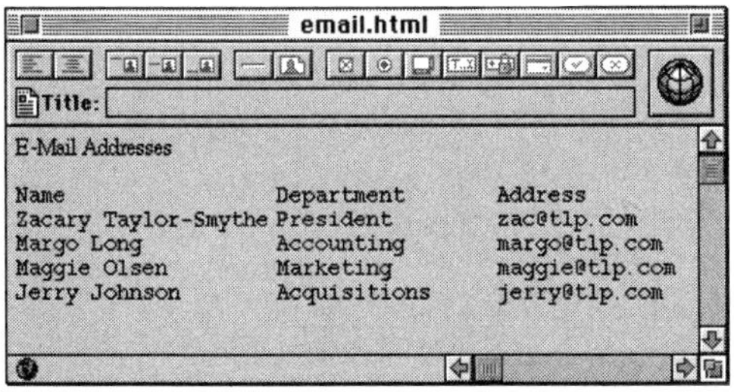

Figure 34a. *A table created with the Preformatted format and tabs may look fine when viewed in PageMill…*

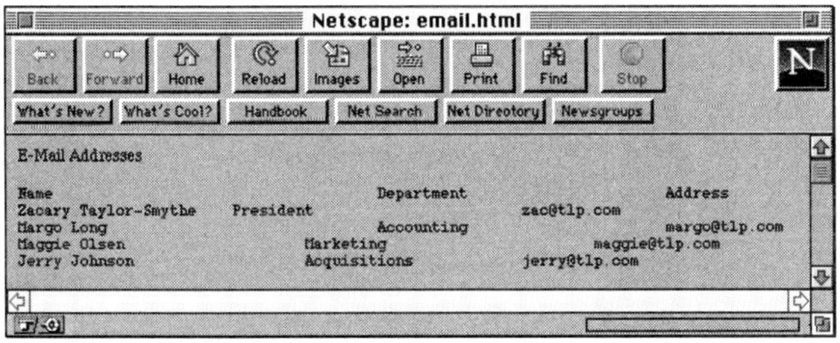

Figure 34a. *…but look at how Netscape Navigator displays it!*

✔ Tips

- Do not use tab characters instead of space characters to create tables. Not all Web browsers use the same amount of space between tab stops (and many do not recognize tabs characters at all). A preformatted table created with tabs may not look right when viewed with a Web browser. This is illustrated in **Figures 34a** and **34b**.
- Since PageMill does not yet support HTML table tags, the Preformatted format is the best way to create and display tabular data with PageMill. If you are familiar with HTML, however, you can use the Raw HTML character style to enter codes to create more complex tables. I tell you about using Raw HTML in **Chapter 9**.

To remove the Preformatted format

1. Select the paragraph(s) from which you want to remove the Preformatted format.
2. Choose Paragraph from the Format menu (see **Figure 14**).

   or

   Press Option ⌘ P.

The Preformatted format is removed from the selection.

About the Address Format

Often, one of the last lines in a Web page is the page author's name, e-mail address, page revision date, or copyright notice. PageMill provides the Address format for formatting this kind of information.

To apply the Address format

1. Select all or part of the paragraph(s) to which you want to apply the Address format (see **Figure 35**).
2. Choose Address from the Format menu (see **Figure 7**).

   or

   Press [Option][⌘][A].

The selected paragraph(s) change accordingly. As you can see in **Figure 36**, Address format includes italic style.

Figure 35. *Select the paragraph(s) to which you want to apply the Address format.*

Figure 36. *The Address format applies an italic style to text.*

✔ Tip

- You cannot remove italic style from the Address format. I tell you about character styles in **Chapter 3**.

To remove the Address format

1. Select all or part of the paragraph(s) from which you want to remove the Address format.
2. Choose Paragraph from the Format menu (see **Figure 14**).

   or

   Press [Option][⌘][P].

Address formatting is removed.

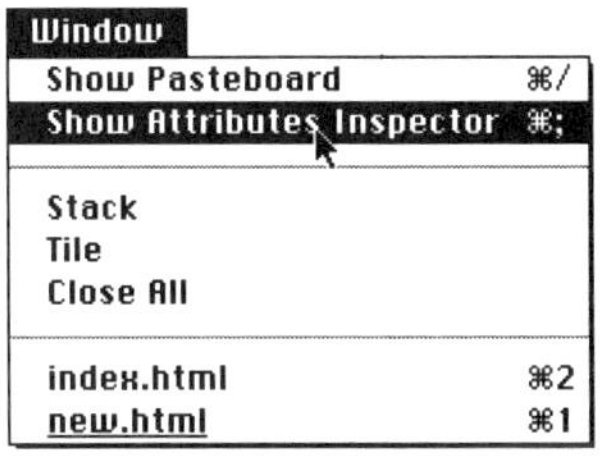

Figure 37. *Choose Show Attributes Inspector from the Window menu.*

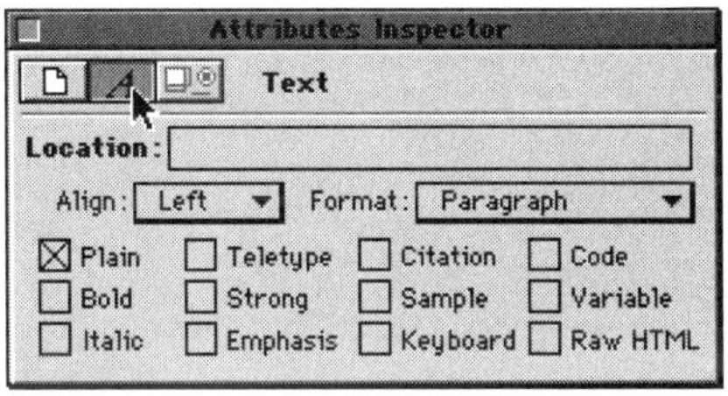

Figure 38. *When you click the Text button on the Attributes Inspector's button bar, you get access to text formatting options.*

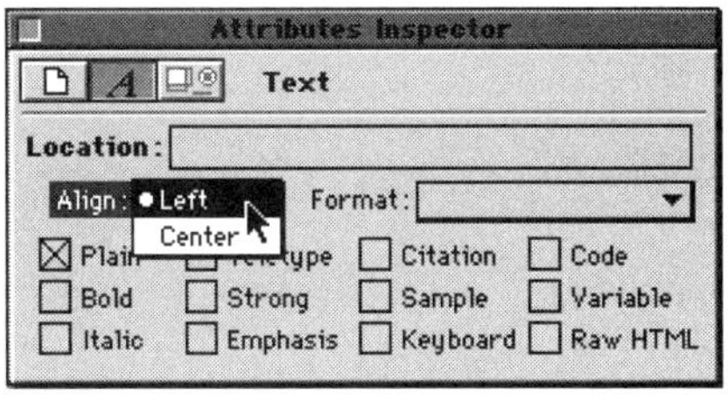

Figure 39a. *The Align pop-up menu offers both alignment options…*

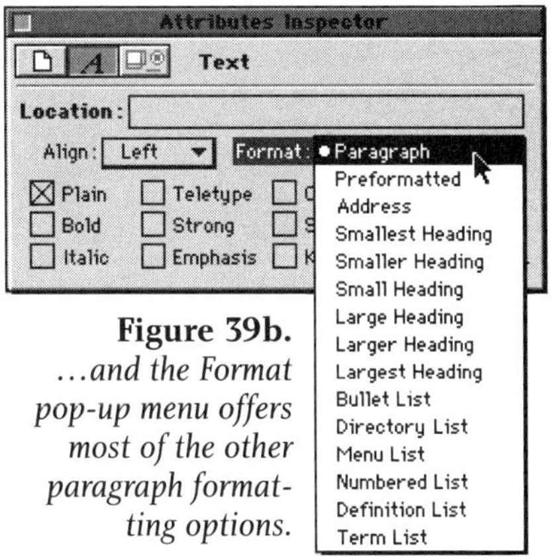

Figure 39b. *…and the Format pop-up menu offers most of the other paragraph formatting options.*

About the Attributes Inspector's Paragraph Formatting Options

The Attributes Inspector offers another way to apply and remove most paragraph formats. Rather than use menu commands, buttons, or Command key equivalents, you can select paragraph(s) and choose options from the Attributes Inspector's two pop-up menus (see **Figures 39a** and **39b**).

To apply formats with the Attributes Inspector

1. If the Attributes Inspector is not displayed, choose Show Attributes Inspector from the Window menu (see **Figure 37**) or press [⌘] [;].
2. If necessary, click the Text button on the Attributes Inspector's button bar (see **Figure 38**) to display the Text options.
3. In the page document window, select the paragraph(s) to which you want to apply a format.
4. In the Attributes Inspector:
   - ▲ Use the Align pop-up menu to select an alignment option (see **Figure 39a**).
   - ▲ Use the Format pop-up menu to select a paragraph format option (see **Figure 39b**).
5. Repeat steps 3 and 4 to apply formats throughout the document.

To change or remove formats with the Attributes Inspector

1. Follow Steps 1 and 2 on the previous page, if necessary, to display the Attributes Inspector and its Text options.
2. In the page document window, select the paragraph(s) from which you want to change or remove formatting.
3. In the Attributes Inspector:
   ▲ Choose the new format you want from the Format pop-up menu.

   or

   ▲ Choose Paragraph from the Format pop-up menu (see **Figure 39b**).

✔ Tips

■ The concepts discussed throughout this chapter also apply when using the Attributes Inspector to apply or remove formats.

■ The Text options of the Attributes Inspector also enables you to apply character styles. I tell you about character styles in **Chapter 3**.

WORKING WITH GRAPHIC IMAGES 5

About Images

One of the best features of the World Wide Web is its ability to support graphics images in formats that can be viewed by Web browsers on all major computer platforms.

Figure 1. *This page uses images for a company logo, a button that links to another page, and a divider line. Although none of these are necessary, they add visual appeal to the page and help establish and maintain a corporate identity.*

As shown in **Figure 1**, images can be used a variety of different ways on a Web page:

- To illustrate something with a photograph, drawing, or diagram.
- To enhance the design of the page with an illustration, company logo, or other graphic element.
- To provide a link to another page, a file, an e-mail address, or other Internet reference. I tell you about creating links in **Chapter 6**.

PageMill makes it easy to use images on your pages.

✔ Tips

- By using image-maps, a single image can provide links to multiple pages. I tell you about links in **Chapter 6**.
- In order to view an image on a Web page, the image file must be loaded into the Web browser. The speed at which the image loads depends on the speed of the user's connection to the Internet. Direct connections will have fast transfers while modem connections will have much slower transfers. To avoid frustrating delays when loading your pages, try to keep the sizes of the image files small.

About Image Formats

Web browsers can read and display two common image formats:

- **GIF** is an 8-bit (256-color) format that is widely used on the Web.
- **JPEG** is a 24-bit (16 million-color) format that uses compression to reduce file size. Although some image quality may be lost in the compression process, it may be a better format for color-rich images like photographs.

✔ Tips

- When you add an image to a page file by pasting or dragging it in, PageMill automatically saves it in GIF format. When you add an image with the Insert Image button or its Command key equivalent, PageMill saves the file in GIF format unless it's a JPEG file; if it's a JPEG file, PageMill retains that format.
- PageMill saves all image files in the folder you specified in the Preferences dialog box (see **Figure 2**). I tell you about Preferences in **Chapter 1**.
- If you prefer JPEG format, you can save images into PageMill's images folder in JPEG format before you use them in PageMill. Many graphics applications support JPEG, including Photoshop, DeBabelizer, and GraphicConverter. Once saved, you can use the Insert Image button or Command key equivalent to insert JPEG images in your pages without converting them.

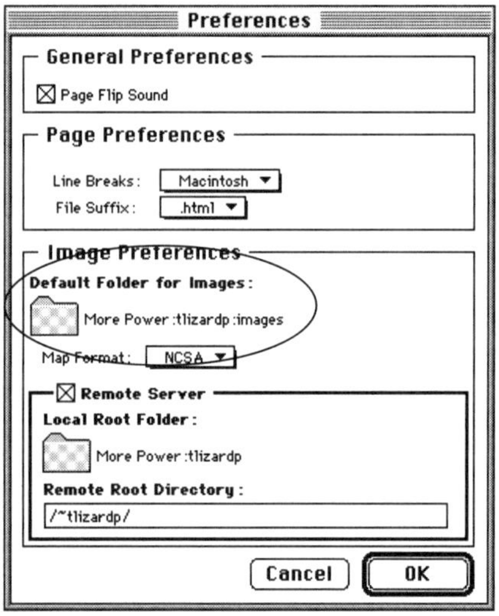

Figure 2. *Use the Preferences dialog box to tell PageMill where to save image files.*

Figure 3. *Select the image you want to copy. In this illustration, a Photoshop graphic is selected.*

Figure 4. *Choose Copy from the Edit menu. Since the image is in Photoshop, the Copy command is on Photoshop's Edit menu.*

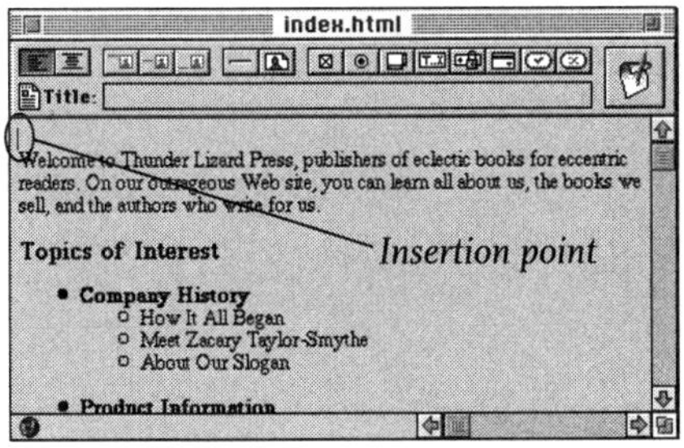

Figure 5. *Position the insertion point where you want the image to appear in the PageMill document.*

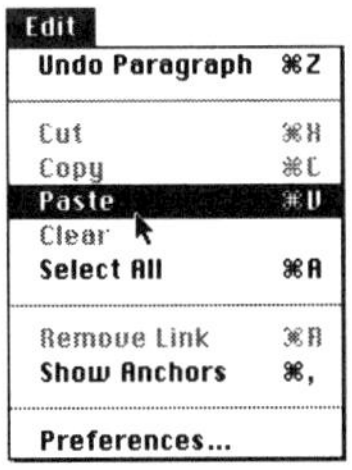

Figure 6. *Choose Paste from the Edit menu. Since the image is being pasted into PageMill, the Paste command is on PageMill's Edit menu.*

About Inserting Images

PageMill offers several ways to insert image files:

- Use the Copy and Paste commands.
- Drag it from another document window.
- Drag it from the Pasteboard.
- Use the Insert Image button or its Command key equivalent.

To insert an image with the Copy & Paste commands

1. Open the document containing the image you want to use.
2. Select the image you want to copy (see **Figure 3**).
3. Choose Copy from the Edit menu (see **Figure 4**) or press ⌘C.

   The image is copied to the Clipboard.
4. Open or activate the PageMill document in which you want to insert the image.
5. Position the insertion point where you want the copied image to appear (see **Figure 5**).
6. Choose Paste from the Edit menu (see **Figure 6**) or press ⌘V.

   A copy of the image in the Clipboard is pasted into the PageMill document at the insertion point (see **Figure 7**).

Figure 7. *The image appears at the insertion point.*

To insert an image by dragging

1. Open the document containing the image you want to use.
2. Open the PageMill document in which you plan to use the image.
3. Arrange the two document windows so that you can see both of their contents (see **Figure 8**).
4. Activate the window containing the image you want to use.
5. Select the image you want to copy (see **Figure 9**).
6. Position the mouse pointer in the *middle* of the selected image. (If the image has selection handles, be sure that you *don't* position the mouse pointer on one of the handles.)
7. Press the mouse button down and drag the image out of its window and into the PageMill document window. As you drag, a dotted line box the same size as the image moves along with the mouse pointer. A blinking insertion point indicates where the text will go when you let go of the mouse button. You can see all this in **Figure 10**.
8. When the blinking insertion point is in the proper position, release the mouse button. The image is copied from its window to the PageMill window (see **Figure 11**).

✔ Tips

- In order for this to work, the image's creator application must support drag and drop editing.
- As you can imagine, this technique works between PageMill windows, too.

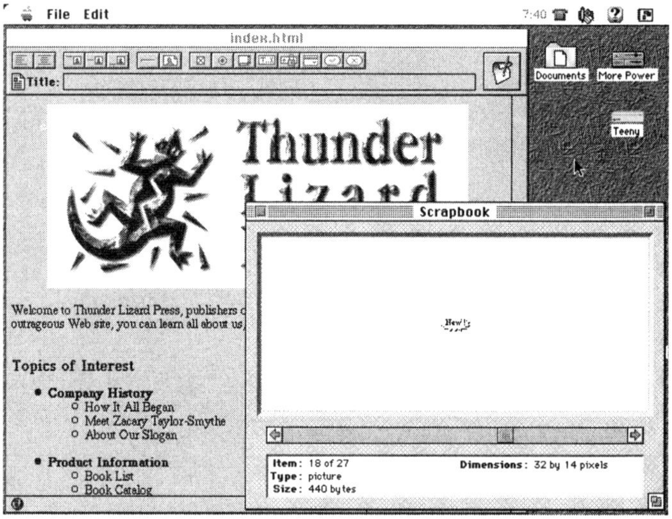

Figure 8. *Arrange the two windows so you can see the contents of both of them.*

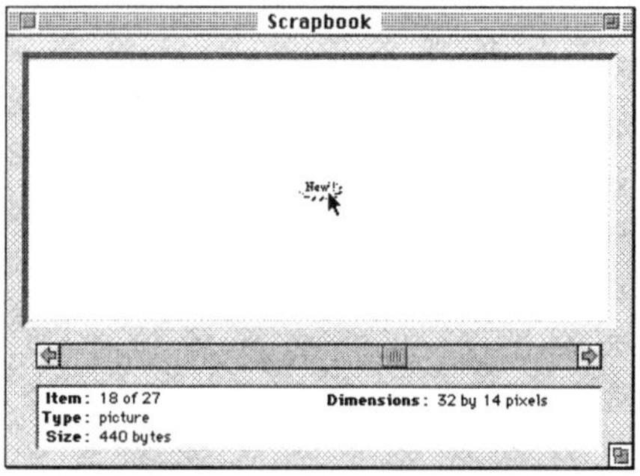

Figure 9. *Select the image you want to copy. Since the image in this example is in the Scrapbook, displaying it selects it.*

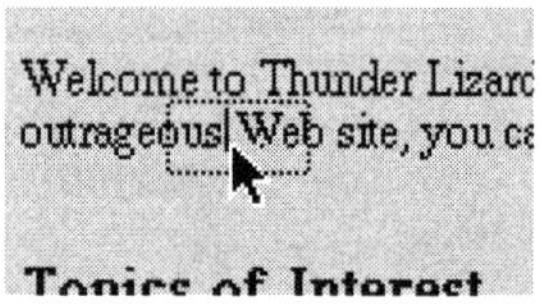

Figure 10. *As you drag, the image's outline appears at the mouse pointer and insertion point.*

Figure 11. *When you let go of the mouse button, the image appears.*

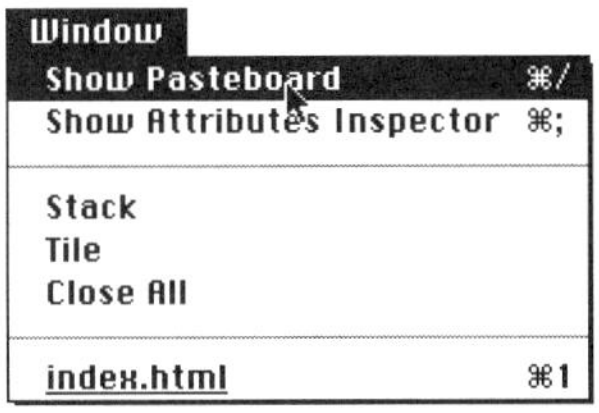

Figure 12. *To display the Pasteboard, choose Show Pasteboard from the Window menu.*

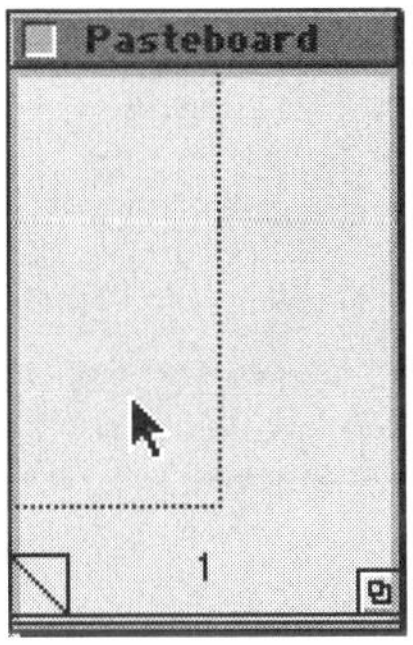

Figure 13. *The image outline moves with the mouse pointer to the Pasteboard.*

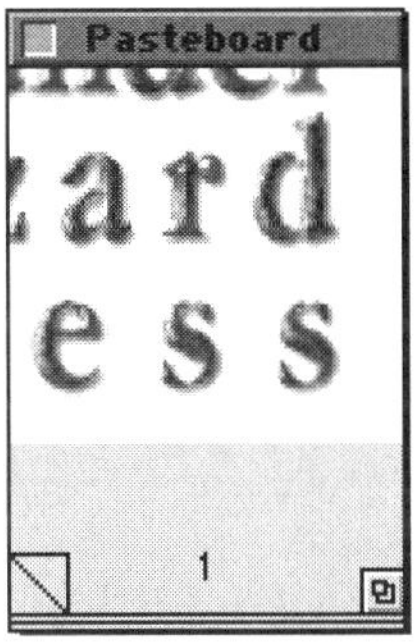

Figure 14. *When you release the mouse button, the image appears on the Pasteboard.*

Figure 15. *Drag the size box in the lower right corner of the Pasteboard to resize it.*

Figure 16. *You can place several items on the Pasteboard. When using an item, be sure to position the mouse pointer right on it.*

To copy an image to the Pasteboard

1. If the Pasteboard is not showing, choose Show Pasteboard from the Window menu (see **Figure 12**) or press ⌘/.
2. Use the drag and drop techniques discussed on the previous page to drag an image from a PageMill document window to the Pasteboard window.
3. When a selection border appears around the inside of the Pasteboard window (see **Figure 13**), release the mouse button.

A copy of the image is placed on the Pasteboard (see **Figure 14**).

✔ Tips

- You can resize the Pasteboard by dragging its size box (see **Figure 15**).
- Although the Pasteboard has only five pages, you can copy more than one item to each page (see **Figure 16**).
- I tell you more about working with the Pasteboard in **Chapters 1** and **2**.

To insert an image from the Pasteboard

1. Position the mouse pointer on the Pasteboard item you want to use (see **Figure 16**).
2. Use the drag and drop techniques discussed on the previous page to move (just drag) or copy (hold down Option while dragging) the item from the Pasteboard into position in a PageMill document.

✔ Tip

- Dragging an item off the Pasteboard is the only way to remove it from the Pasteboard.

To insert an image with the Insert Image button

1. Position the insertion point where you want the image to appear (see **Figure 17**).
2. Click the Insert Image button on the button bar. 

   or

   Press [⌘][Control][2].

   A standard Open dialog box appears (see **Figure 18**).
3. Locate and select the file containing the image you want to insert.
4. Click Open or press [Return] or [Enter].

The image in the file you selected appears in the PageMill window (see **Figure 19**).

Figure 17. *Position the insertion point where you want the image to appear.*

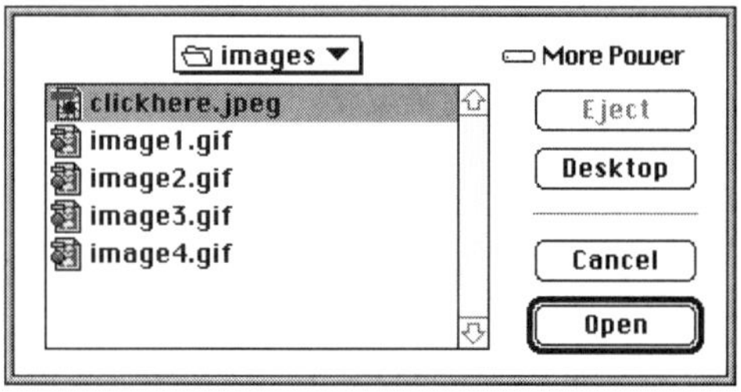

Figure 18. *Use the Open dialog box to locate and open the image you want to insert.*

Figure 19. *The image is inserted into the document.*

✔ Tips

- Only files of types GIF, JPEG, or PICT will appear in the Open dialog box when you use the Insert Image button or its Command key equivalent.
- If the file you insert is a GIF or JPEG file, PageMill does not resave it. Instead, it inserts a reference to the file in the PageMill document.
- If the file you insert is a PICT file, PageMill converts the file to a GIF file and saves it in the images folder you specified in the Preferences dialog box (see **Figure 2**).
- Another way to insert a GIF, JPEG, or PICT file into a PageMill document is by dragging its Finder icon into the document's window (see **Figure 20**). Consult the "To insert an image by dragging" section earlier in this chapter for specific information about drag and drop techniques. The tips above regarding file formats apply.

Figure 20. *You can drag the icon for a GIF, JPEG, or PICT file right out of a Finder window and into a PageMill document window.*

About the Image Not Found Icon

Figure 21. *When PageMill can't find an image file it needs to display, it displays the Image Not Found icon.*

If PageMill cannot locate the image file for an image on a page, it displays an Image Not Found icon (see **Figure 21**). To solve this problem, use one of the following techniques:

- Remove the icon and reinsert the image using one of the techniques on the previous pages.
- Double-click the icon to display an Open dialog box (see **Figure 18**) and use that to locate and open the image on disk.

✔ Tip

- To avoid this problem, make sure all images you insert, whether by pasting, dragging, or using the Insert Image button, are in a folder within the Local Root Folder you specified in the Preferences dialog box. (see **Figure 2**). I tell you about the Local Root Folder in **Chapter 1**.

About Selecting Images

In order to modify, copy, move, or delete an image, you need to select it.

To select an image

Click the image you want to select.

A selection box appears around the image and three resizing handles appear (see **Figure 22**).

Figure 22. *When you select an image, a selection box and handles appear around it.*

To deselect an image

Click inside the document window anywhere other than on the selected image.

The selection box and handles disappear.

About Copying, Moving, & Deleting Images

Like text, once an image is in a PageMill document, it can be moved or copied a number of different ways:

- The Copy and Paste commands let you copy an image from one place and paste it in another.
- The Cut and Paste commands let you cut an image from one place and paste it in another, thus moving the original image.
- Drag and drop editing lets you move or copy a selected image by simply dragging it.
- The Pasteboard lets you store images that you can drag into a document window.

I discuss the first three techniques for text in **Chapter 2**. They work the same way for images. I discuss using the Pasteboard for images earlier in this chapter.

To delete an image

1. Select the image you want to delete.
2. Press Delete.

   or

   Choose Clear from the Edit menu (see **Figure 23**).

The image disappears.

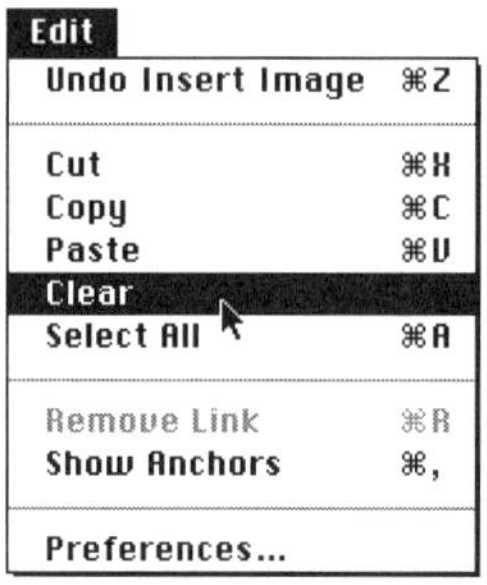

Figure 23. *Choosing Clear from the Edit menu deletes whatever is selected, including images.*

✔ Tip

- When you delete an image, its image file remains on disk, even if the file was created by PageMill and saved into the Images folder.

About Resizing Images

Once an image has been inserted in a PageMill document, it can be resized as needed by either dragging its resizing handles or using the Attributes Inspector.

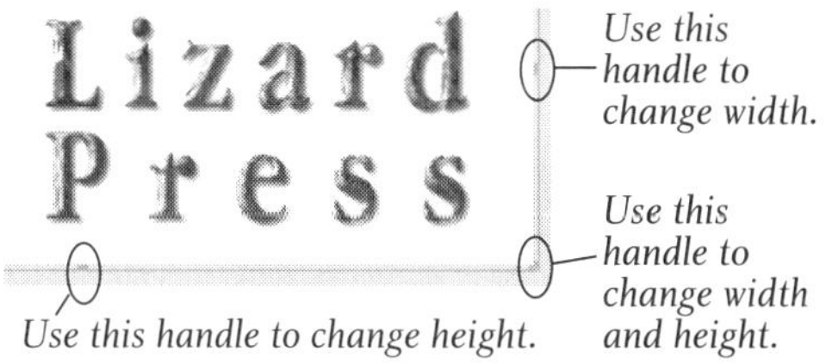

Figure 24. *Choose a resizing handle based on the way you want to resize the image.*

To resize an image by dragging

1. Select the image you want to resize.
2. Position the mouse pointer over one of its resizing handles (see **Figure 24**):
   - ▲ To change its width, position the mouse pointer over the handle on the right side of the image.
   - ▲ To change its height, position the mouse pointer over the handle on the bottom of the image.
   - ▲ To change its width and height, position the mouse pointer over the handle in the bottom right corner of the image.
3. Press the mouse button down and drag. As you drag, an outline indicates the size of the image when you release the mouse button (see **Figure 25**).
4. Release the mouse button. The image resizes (see **Figure 26**).

Figure 25. *As you drag, an outline indicates the final size of the image.*

Figure 26. *When you release the mouse button, the image resizes.*

✔ Tip

- ■ To change both the width and height of an image without changing their proportions, press Shift and hold it down while you press down the mouse button and drag. Release the mouse button first, then release Shift.

To resize an image with the Attributes Inspector

1. If the Attributes Inspector is not displayed, choose Show Attributes Inspector from the Window menu (see **Figure 27**) or press ⌘;.
2. In the page document window, select the image you want to resize.
3. If necessary, click the Object button on the Attributes Inspector's button bar (see **Figure 28**) to display the Image options.
4. To change the width or height to an exact pixel measurement or percentage of the original image, make sure the Scale to Height and Scale to Width check boxes are turned off, then choose Pixels or Percent from the Width and Height pop-up menus (see **Figure 29**) and enter a value in the Width and Height Edit boxes.

   or

   To resize an image proportionally, turn off either the Scale to Height or Scale to Width check box, then choose Pixels or Percent from the pop-up menu beside it and enter a value in the opposite edit box (see **Figure 30**).

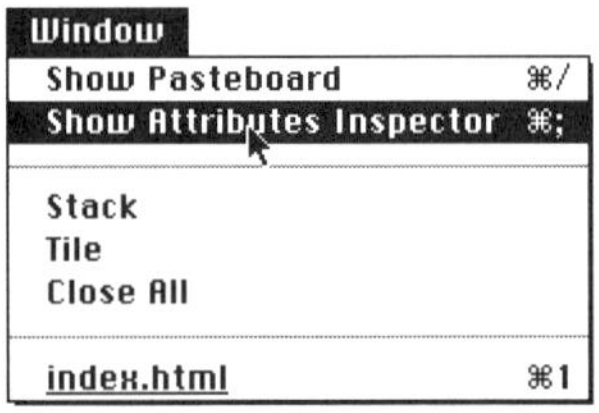

Figure 27. *Choose Show Attributes Inspector from the Window menu.*

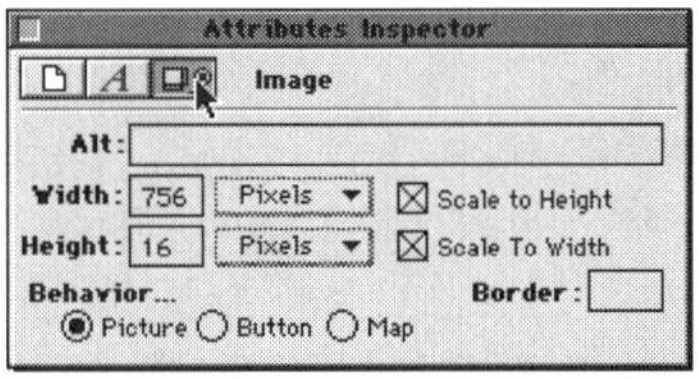

Figure 28. *With an image selected, click the Object button in the Attributes Inspector to display the Image options.*

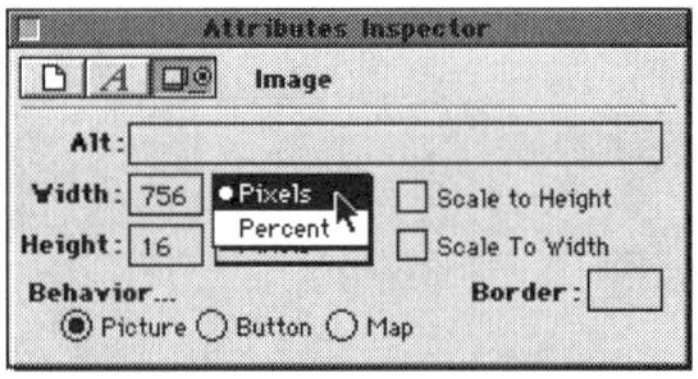

Figure 29. *You can resize an image based on a pixel measurement or percent of the original image.*

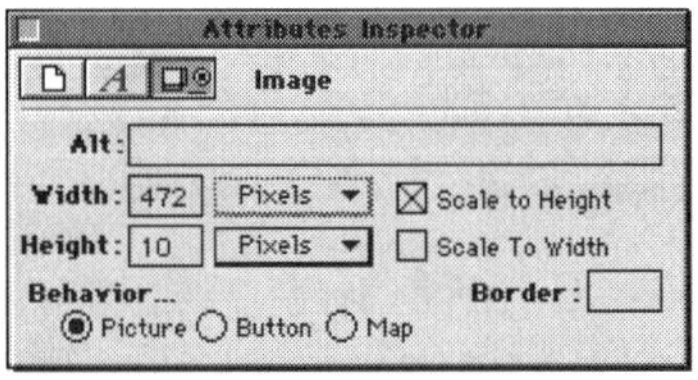

Figure 30. *This example shows how the image was resized proportionally by turning on only the Scale to Height check box and entering a new value in the Height edit box.*

✔ Tips

- An image must be selected before you click the Object button on the Attributes Inspector button bar to display the Image options.
- You must press Return or Enter to accept an entry in an Attributes Inspector edit box. If you fail to do so, the contents of the edit box may change back to its original value.
- Make sure the Behavior radio button is set to Picture unless the image will be used as a button or an image map. I tell you about buttons in **Chapter 7** and about image maps in **Chapter 6**.

Figure 31. *Select the image.*

Figure 32. *Here's the image from* Figure 31 *with the Center Align Text button selected.*

About Image Alignment

Images can be aligned two ways:

- Use paragraph alignment to adjust the position of an image between the right and left sides of the window. This is effective when working with an image that is all by itself in a paragraph. (I tell you more about paragraph alignment in **Chapter 4**.)
- Use image alignment to adjust the position of an image in relation to the text within its paragraph. This is effective when the image is in the same line as text.

✔ Tip

- By default, text alignment is set to left aligned and image alignment is set to bottom aligned.

To align an image horizontally

1. Select the image you want to align (see **Figure 31**).
2. Click the appropriate text alignment button on the button bar:
   - ▲ Click the Left Align Text button or press ⌘ Control ← to align the image with the left side of the window. 
   - ▲ Click the Center Align Text button or press ⌘ Control → to center the image in the window. 

The image shifts (see **Figure 32**).

To align an image vertically

1. Select the image you want to align (see **Figure 33**).
2. Click the appropriate image alignment button on the button bar:
   - ▲ Click the Top Align Image button or press ⌘ Control ↑ to align the top of the image with the text.
   - ▲ Click the Center Align Image button to align the center of the image with the text. The Command key equivalents are ⌘ Control ↑ if the image is top-aligned when you change it and ⌘ Control ↓ if the image is bottom aligned when you change it.
   - ▲ Click the Bottom Align Image button or press ⌘ Control ↓ to align the bottom of the image with the text.

The Image or text shifts (see **Figure 34**).

Figure 33. *Select the image.*

Figure 34. *Here's the image from Figure 33 with the Center Align Image button selected.*

About Image View

Image view (see **Figure 35**) gives you access to several image-related features:

- ■ Make a certain color within the image transparent so the background shows through it.
- ■ Create an image map so that clicking "hot spots" in the image displays another page. I tell you more about image maps in **Chapter 6**.
- ■ Save an image as an interlaced GIF, which loads into a Web browser with a Venetian blind effect.

Figure 35. *Double-click an image to open and work with it in Image view.*

To work with an image in Image view

Double-click the image with which you want to work.

An Image view window containing the image appears (see **Figure 35**).

To make a color transparent

1. In the Image view window, click the Transparency tool.  The mouse pointer, when moved atop the image, changes to the Transparency tool icon (see **Figure 36**).
2. Click any color you want to make transparent. The image changes so you can see the Image view background through the color you made transparent (see **Figure 37**).

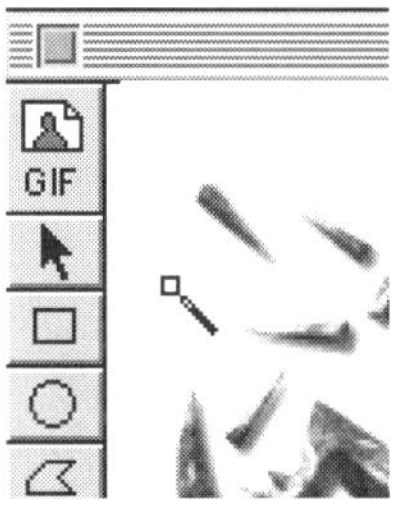

Figure 36. *When you click the Transparency tool, the mouse pointer changes.*

Figure 37. *In this example, the white background was turned transparent.*

✔ Tips

- The Transparency tool is available only if the image in the Image view windows is in GIF format.
- Only one color can be transparent.
- When you make a color transparent, that information is saved with the image file so it is transparent no matter what page it is used in.
- To restore the transparent color, use the Transparency tool to click the transparent area. The color returns.
- Use the Transparency tool to make the background color of an image (usually white) transparent. This greatly improves the appearance of an image on a large background (see **Figure 38**).
- Combine transparent image backgrounds with page backgrounds to give your pages professional polish. I tell you about page backgrounds in **Chapter 8**.

Figure 38. *Here's what the images inserted throughout this chapter look like with their white backgrounds made transparent.*

To create an interlaced GIF

In the Image view window, click the Interlace Toggle switch.

If you look closely, you'll see that the switch changes so that there are horizontal lines across the image on its icon. This means that the image, when saved, will be saved as an interlaced GIF.

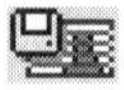

✔ Tips

- The Interlace Toggle switch appears only if the image in the Image view windows is in GIF format.
- To change an interlaced GIF back to a regular GIF, click the Interlace Toggle switch to remove the horizontal lines from the image on its icon.
- Interlaced GIFs are good for large images that could take more than a few seconds to load. The entire GIF loads as a blurred image that progressively clears until it is completed loaded.

To save Image view changes

1. If necessary, activate the Image view window.
2. Choose Save from the File menu (see **Figure 39**).

   or

   Press [⌘][S].

Any changes you made to the image while working in Image view are saved.

To close the Image view window

Choose Close from the File menu (see **Figure 39**).

or

Press [⌘][W].

or

Click the Image view window's close box.

Figure 39. *Use commands under the File menu to Save and Close an Image view window.*

Figure 40. *If you try to close an Image view window before saving changes, a dialog box like this appears.*

✔ Tip

- If you don't save changes to an Image view window before closing the window, a dialog box like the one in **Figure 40** will appear.
  - ▲ Click Save or press [Return] or [Enter] to save changes before closing the window.
  - ▲ Click Don't Save to close the window without saving changes.
  - ▲ Click Cancel to dismiss the dialog box without closing the window.

Figure 41. *Enter alternate text in the Alt edit box and press* Return.

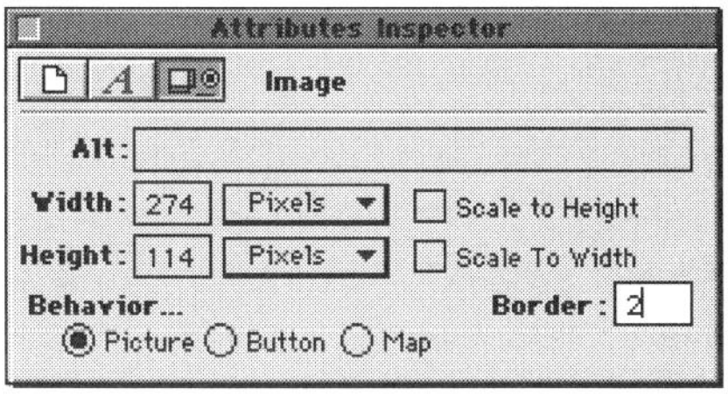

Figure 42. *Enter a width for the border in pixels and press* Return.

Figure 43. *An image with a 2-pixel thick border.*

About Other Image Options

Using the Attributes Inspector, you can change other image options:

- Specify alternate text.
- Add a border to an image (see **Figure 43**).

To specify alternate text or add a border

1. If the Attributes Inspector is not displayed, choose Show Attributes Inspector from the Window menu (see **Figure 27**) or press ⌘;.
2. In the page document window, select the image for which you want to specify alternate text.
3. If necessary, click the Object button on the Attributes Inspector's button bar (see **Figure 28**) to display the Image options.
4. To specify alternate text, click in the Alt edit box to activate it and enter the text you want to appear (see **Figure 41**). Then press Return or Enter to complete the entry.

   or

   To add a border, click in the Border edit box to activate it and enter a border width, in pixels (see **Figure 42**). Then press Return or Enter to complete the entry.

✔ Tips

- Alternate text is displayed when the page is viewed with a text browser or a browser with the automatic image loading feature turned off.
- You must press Return or Enter to complete the entry. If you don't the entry will be lost when you click outside the Attributes Inspector window.
- To remove alternate text or a border, follow steps 1 through 3 above. Then clear the contents of the Alt or Border edit box and press Return or Enter.
- If you clear the contents of the Border edit box for an image that is used as a link, its blue link border disappears. I tell you about links in **Chapter 6**.

About Horizontal Rules

A horizontal rule is a graphic element that is part of HTML. Its HTML code is interpreted by the web browser and displayed as a horizontal line. No special graphic file is required.

To add a horizontal rule

1. Position the insertion point where you want the horizontal rule to appear (see **Figure 44**).
2. Click the Insert Horizontal Rule button on the button bar.

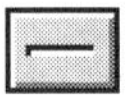

or

Press [⌘][Control][1].

The horizontal rule appears (see **Figure 45**).

To format a horizontal rule

1. Click the horizontal rule to select it. A selection box and resizing handles appear (see **Figure 46**).
2. Drag a resizing handle to change the length or thickness (or both) for the horizontal line.

or

Click the Object button on the Attributes Inspector to display Horizontal Rule options (see **Figure 47**). Enter a thickness, in points, in the Size edit box and a width, as a percentage of the page width, in the Width edit box. Press [Return] or [Enter] after each entry so PageMill accepts it.

Figure 48 shows an example of 5-point, 75% wide horizontal rule.

To remove a horizontal rule

1. Click the horizontal rule to select it.
2. Press [Delete].

Figure 44. *Position the insertion point where you want the horizontal rule to appear.*

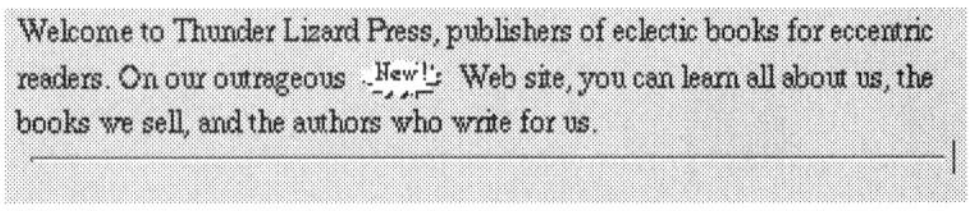

Figure 45. *When you click the Insert Horizontal Rule button a line appears.*

Figure 46. *To modify the horizontal rule, begin by selecting it.*

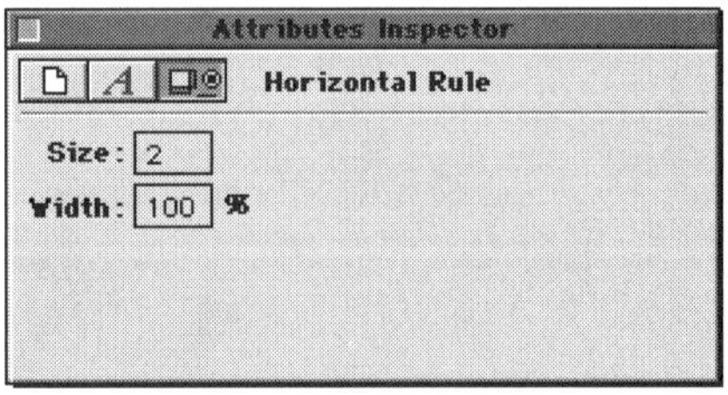

Figure 47. *The Horizontal Rule options in the Attributes Inspector window let you specify measurements for the thickness and width of a rule.*

Figure 48. *Here's the horizontal rule from* Figure 45, *fattened up and shortened.*

✔ Tips

- You cannot make a horizontal rule's length exceed the page width if you resize it by dragging a resizing handle.
- You can use the text alignment buttons to left align or center a horizontal rule.

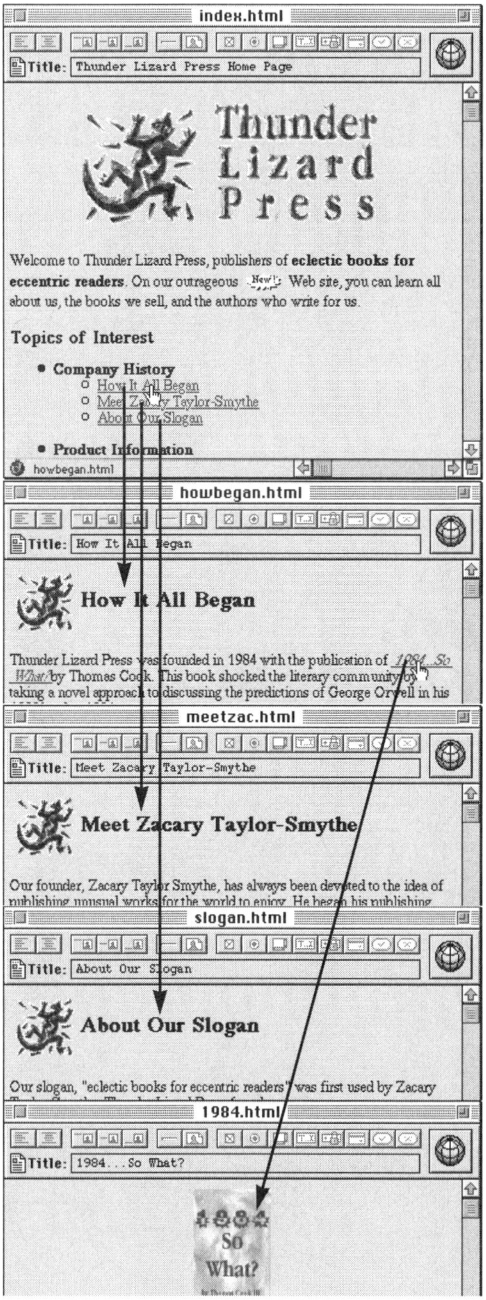

About Links

The real power of World Wide Web publishing lies in its ability to link your Web pages to each other and to other pages and references anywhere on the Internet. When properly set up, someone browsing your pages can click a hypertext or graphic link to display another page—even one that's on a server halfway across the world! **Figure 1** shows an example of links between several pages on the same site.

When working with links, there are two kinds of documents:

- The *source* document is the one containing the clickable link.
- The *destination* or *referenced* document is the one that is displayed when you click a link.

A link works by including the address or URL (Uniform Resource Locator) of the destination page within HTML codes associated with text or an image on the source page. While that may sound complex, with PageMill, it's easy since PageMill automatically prepares the HTML codes for you.

✔ Tips

- You can recognize linked text or graphics on a Web page by the colored underline or border around it.
- Although the default link color is blue, it can be changed. I tell you how in **Chapter 8**.

Figure 1. *This example shows several links from a "Home" page to other pages on the same site.*

About Page Icons

PageMill stores information about a page location in the Page icon near the top left corner of the window (see **Figure 2**). By dragging the Page icon, you create anchors and links.

Page icon

Figure 2. *You create links and anchors by dragging the Page icon.*

✔ Tip

- If the page has not yet been saved, the Page icon area will be empty (see **Figure 3**). You must save the page before you can drag its Page icon.

Empty Page icon

Figure 3. *If a document has not yet been saved, its Page icon area will be empty.*

About Anchors

Normally, when you create a link to a page, clicking the link displays the top of the page. When you create a link to an *anchor*, however, clicking the link displays a specific location on the page.

✔ Tip

- Anchors are especially useful on long pages. By creating a page table of contents at the top of the page with links to anchors placed at topics throughout the page, you provide easy access to topics without a lot of scrolling.

To create an anchor

1. Drag the Page icon into the page. As you drag, an outline of the icon moves with your mouse pointer. A blinking insertion point indicates where the anchor will appear when you release the mouse button. You can see all this in **Figure 4**.
2. When the insertion point is in the desired position, release the mouse button. If PageMill is set to display anchors, an anchor icon appears (see **Figure 5**).

Figure 4. *Drag the Page icon into the document window and release it where you want to place an anchor.*

Figure 5. *The anchor icon looks like a little anchor.*

Creating an Anchor

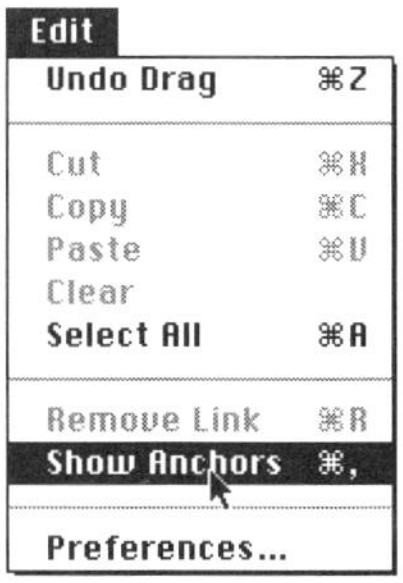

Figure 6. *If anchors aren't displayed, choose Show Anchors from the Edit menu.*

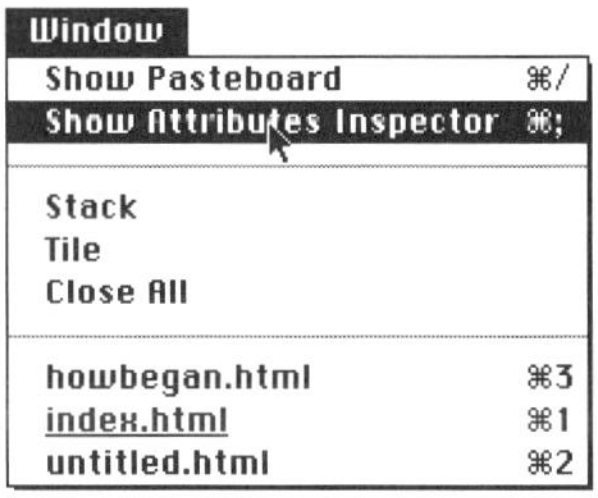

Figure 7. *Choose Show Attributes Inspector from the Window menu.*

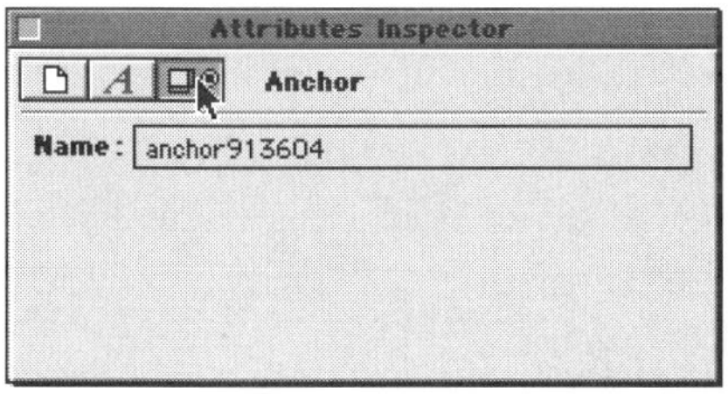

Figure 8. *An anchor's name appears in the Anchor options in the Attributes Inspector.*

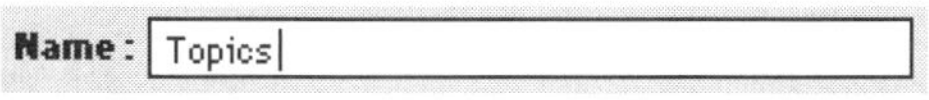

Figure 9. *Type the anchor name in the Name edit box and press* Return.

✔ Tips

- It is not necessary to name the anchors you create. You may find it helpful, however, if you plan to edit the HTML code PageMill creates. I tell you about editing HTML in **Chapter 9**.
- If you delete an anchor that is referenced by a link, the link will no longer function.

To display anchors

Choose Show Anchors from the Edit menu (see **Figure 6**).

or

Press ⌘ ,.

✔ Tips

- Anchors do not appear in Preview view.
- To hide anchors, choose Hide Anchors from the Edit menu or press ⌘ ,.

To move an anchor

Drag the anchor to a new position within the page. Any links that reference the anchor will automatically reference it in its new position.

To name an anchor

1. Select the anchor you want to name (see **Figure 5**).
2. If necessary, choose Show Attributes Inspector from the Window menu (see **Figure 7**) or press ⌘ ; to display the Attributes Inspector.
3. Click the Object button on the Attributes Inspector's button bar to display Anchor options (see **Figure 8**).
4. Click in the Name edit box to activate it and type the name you want to use for the anchor (see **Figure 9**). Press Return or Enter to complete the entry.

To delete an anchor

1. Select the anchor you want to delete (see **Figure 5**).
2. Press Delete. The anchor disappears.

About Adding Links

PageMill offers several methods for adding links to text and images:

- Use drag and drop to create links to pages you create.
- Use copy and paste to copy links on one page to other pages.
- Type a link address into the Link Location Bar or Attributes Inspector.

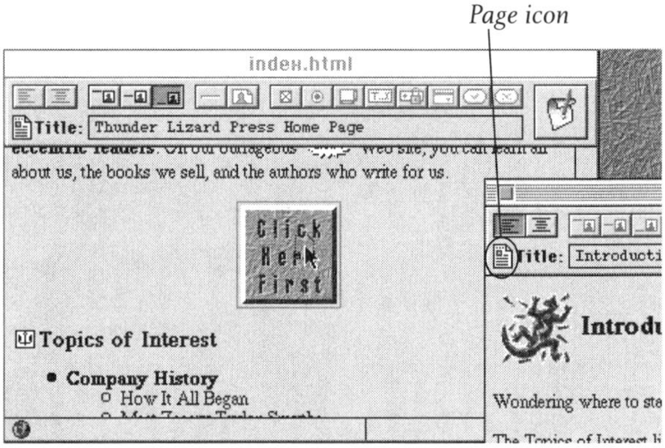

Figure 10. *This example shows a Page icon being dragged onto a selected image.*

To add a link by dragging

1. In the source document, select the text or image that you want to use as a link.
2. Drag the Page icon for the destination document onto the selection (see **Figure 10**).

   or

   Drag the anchor for the destination location onto the selection (see **Figure 11**).

   or

   Drag a selected link onto the selection.

When you release the mouse button, the selection gets a blue underline (if it's text; see **Figure 12**) or a blue border (if it's an image; see **Figure 13**) to indicate that it's a link.

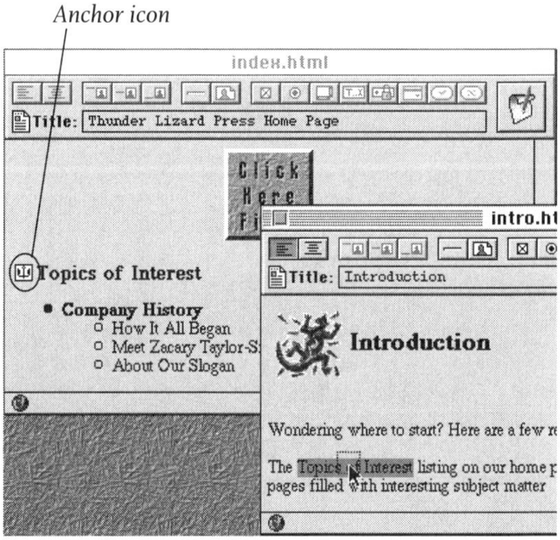

Figure 11. *This example shows an anchor icon being dragged onto selected text.*

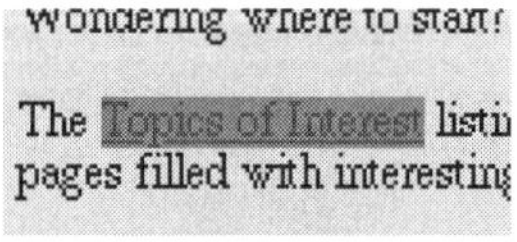

Figure 12. *Here's the linked text right after the anchor was dropped on it in* Figure 11.

Figure 13. *Here's the linked image right after the Page icon was dropped on it in* Figure 10.

✔ Tips

- To select a text link, triple-click it.
- When you select a link, the destination address appears in the Link Location Bar at the bottom of the page window (see **Figure 14**). You can copy the link by dragging the globe icon to another location.
- Selected text on inactive pages appears with a selection border around it (see **Figure 15**).

Figure 14. *When a link is selected, its destination URL appears in the Link Location Bar.*

Figure 15. *A selection on an inactive page appears with a border around it.*

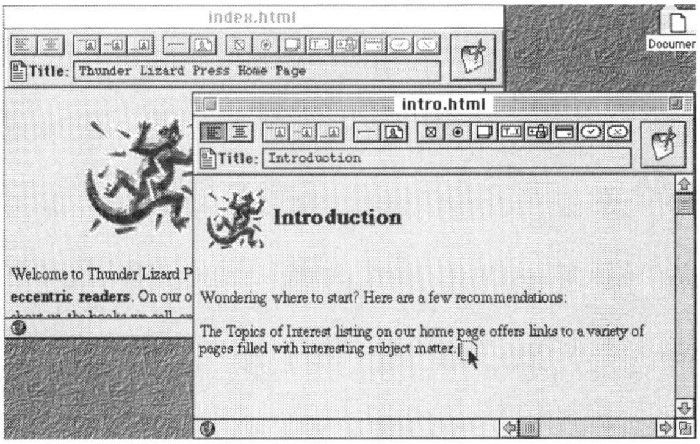

Figure 16. *You can also drag a page icon or anchor onto a page without dropping it on a selection.*

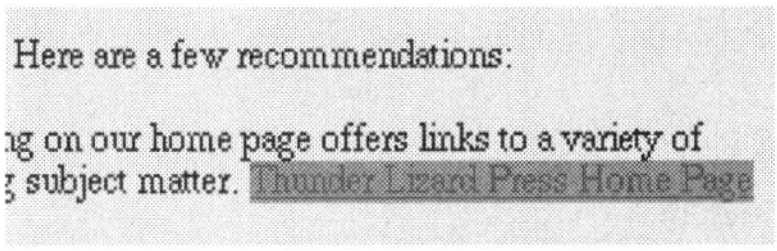

Figure 17. *Here's the link PageMill created from the drag and drop operation in* Figure 16.

Figure 18. *Use the Copy and Paste commands under the Edit menu to copy text or graphics containing links.*

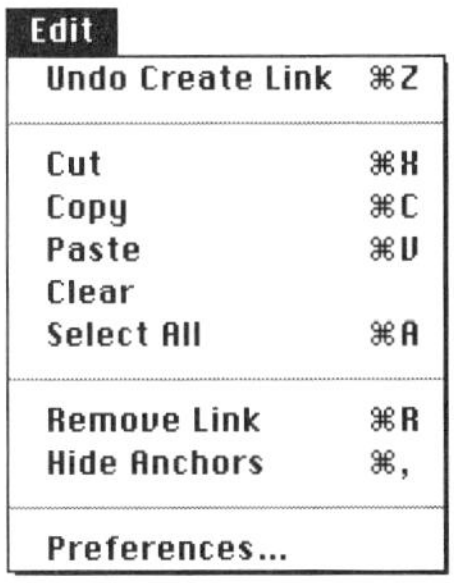

- If you drag a Page icon onto another page without dropping it on a selection (see **Figure 16**), PageMill creates the link for you (see **Figure 17**). You can edit the link just as you would any other text. I tell you how to edit text in **Chapter 2**.
- To create a link to an anchor on the same page by dragging, hold down [⌘] while dragging the anchor into position. This creates a link to the anchor rather than moving the anchor.
  - When you drag text or an image containing a link from the Pasteboard to a document window, the link is pasted into the document along with the text or image. I tell you more about the Pasteboard in **Chapters 1**, **2**, and **5**.

To add a link with the Copy & Paste commands

1. Select the linked text or image (see **Figure 14**).
2. Choose Copy from the Edit menu (see **Figure 18**) or press [⌘][C].
3. Position the insertion point in the document where you want the link to appear.
4. Choose Paste from the Edit menu (see **Figure 18**) or press [⌘][V].

The text or image, including its link, appears at the insertion point.

✔ Tips

- You can also use the Cut and Paste commands to move a link.
- Do not use Copy and Paste to copy an anchor. Doing so will create a duplicate of the anchor, not a link.
- I tell you how to use Copy, Cut, and Paste for text in **Chapter 2** and for images in **Chapter 5**.

To add a link by typing in the Link Location Bar

1. In the source document, select the text or image that you want to use as a link (see **Figure 19**).
2. Click in the Link Location Bar (the area beside the globe icon at the bottom left side of the window) to activate it (see **Figure 20**).
3. Enter the address for the destination (see **Figure 21**) and press Return or Enter to complete the entry.

The selected text or image turns into a link (see **Figure 22**).

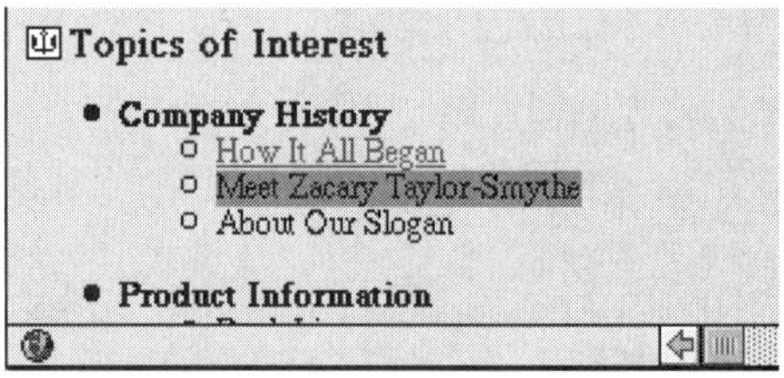

Figure 19. *Select the text you want to use as a link.*

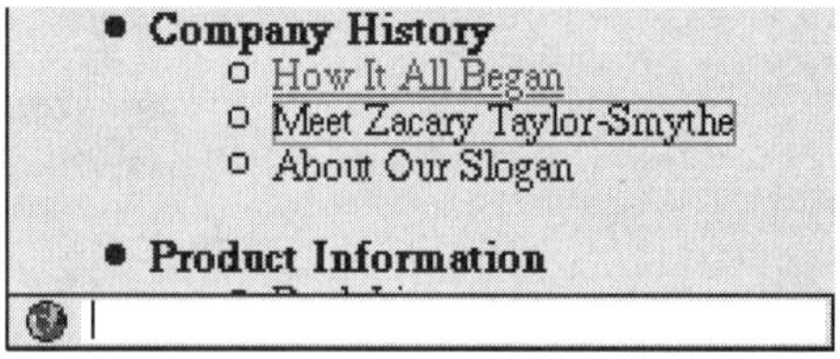

Figure 20. *Activate the Link Location Bar by clicking it.*

Figure 21. *Enter the address for the destination.*

Figure 22. *When you complete the entry, the selected text or image turns into a link.*

To add a link by typing in the Attributes Inspector

1. In the source document, select the text or image that you want to use as a link (see **Figure 19**).
2. If necessary, choose Show Attributes Inspector from the Window menu (see **Figure 7**) or press ⌘; to display the Attributes Inspector.
3. Click the Text button on the Attributes Inspector's button bar to display the Text options (see **Figure 23**).
4. Click in the Location edit box to activate it and type the address. Press Return or Enter to complete the entry.

The selected text or image turns into a link (see **Figure 22**).

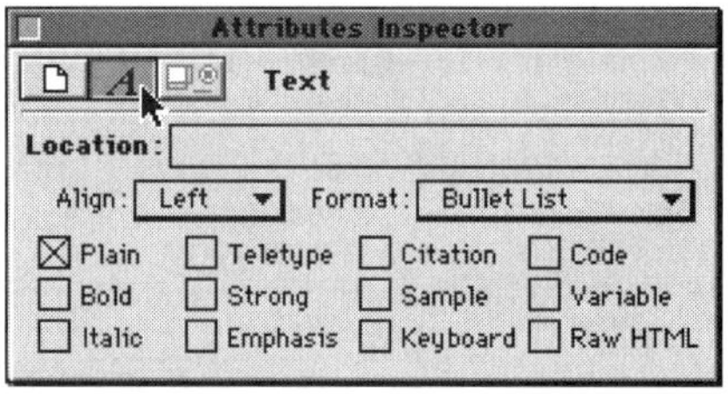

Figure 23. *The Text options of the Attributes Inspector offers another way to create a link.*

✔ Tip

- When typing a link, be sure to enter it correctly. If it has not been entered correctly, it will not work. I tell you how to test links later in **Chapter 9**.

Adding Links by Typing

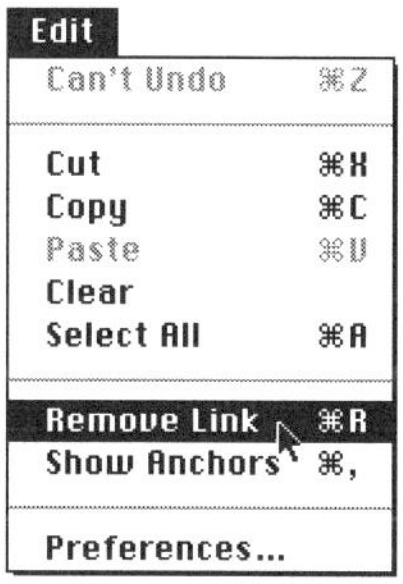

Figure 24. *Use the Remove Link command under the edit menu to remove a link from selected text or images.*

To remove a link

1. Select the text or image containing the link (see **Figure 22**).
2. Choose Remove Link from the Edit menu (see **Figure 24**).

   or

   Press [⌘][R].

   or

   Press [Enter] or click in the Link Location Bar to activate it, press [Delete] to delete its contents, and press [Return] or [Enter] to complete the entry.

   or

   Open the Attributes Inspector, display the Text options, click in the Location edit box to activate it, and press [Delete] to delete its contents. Then press [Return] or [Enter] to complete the entry.

✔ Tips

- Deleting text or an image containing a link also deletes the link.
- Deleting a link does not delete the file that was linked.

About Other Links

When it comes to creating links, you're not limited to linking to the pages you create with PageMill. You can also create links to:

- **Web pages on other sites.** These external links give the people who browse your pages access to more information than you offer.
- **E-mail addresses.** When a link to an e-mail address is clicked, the Web browser opens an addressed an e-mail form (see **Figure 25**) so sending an e-mail message is convenient.
- **Files.** When a link to a file is clicked, the browser software downloads the file to the user's computer. This is a great way to distribute software and information for use offline.

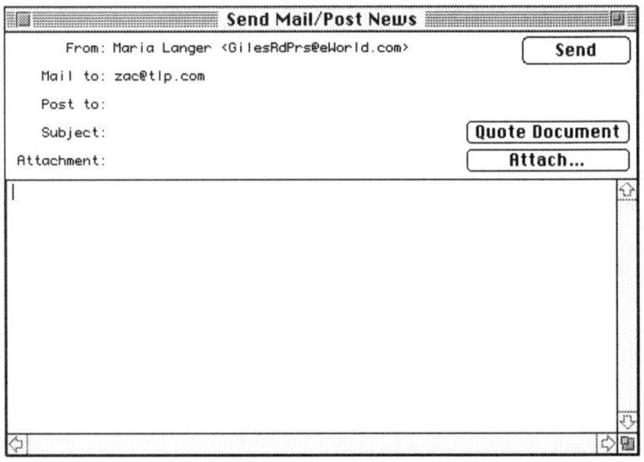

Figure 25. *A link to an e-mail address opens an e-mail form like this one.*

Table 1 provides examples of URLs for external pages, e-mail addresses, and files so you can see exactly how they work.

✔ Tip

- Links to Adobe Acrobat PDF files will display the file when clicked if the user has Adobe Acrobat set up as a "helper" application in the Web browser preferences.

External Pages:

http://www.peachpit.com/

http://www.apple.com/

http://www.adobe.com/

http://www.webcrawler.com/

http://www.intac.com/~gilesrd/

http://www.intac.com/~gilesrd/mlanger/

http://www.sandia.gov/sci_compute/elements.html

E-Mail Addresses:

mailto:info@solutions.apple.com

mailto:GilesRdPrs@eWorld.com

Files:

ftp://solutions.apple.com/README.What.Is.Available

http://www.adobe.com/Software/Acrobat/Macintosh/ACROREAD.MAC.hqx

ftp://ftp.dartmouth.edu/pub/mac/Fetch_3.0.hqx

http://www.intac.com/~gilesrd/mlanger/pdf/PageMillVQS.pdf

Table 1. *Here's a list of real Web pages, e-mail addresses, and files that you can try on your Web pages. Remember, although this list was tested and known to be valid when this book went into production, the Internet is constantly changing—URLs that were valid today, could become invalid tomorrow. If one of these links doesn't work when you try it, you may not be doing anything wrong—that URL may just be out of date.*

Figure 26. *When entering the address for a page that isn't part of your site, you must enter the entire URL.*

✔ Tips

- No matter what kind of link you create, its URL must be entered correctly for it to work.
- Links are often case-sensitive, especially links to files on UNIX servers. Be sure you enter URLs with correct capitalization or the link may not work.
- Check all external links on a regular basis to make sure they're still valid. I tell you how to check external links in **Chapter 9**.

To add a link to a page that is part of another Web site

Follow the steps under "To add a link by typing in the Link Location Bar" or "To add a link by typing in the Attributes Inspector" earlier in this chapter to enter the complete URL for the destination page (see **Figure 26**).

or

Use PageMill to open a page containing the link you want to use (like the Bookmarks.html file created by Netscape) and copy the link from there.

To add a link to an e-mail address

Follow the steps under "To add a link by typing in the Link Location Bar" or "To add a link by typing in the Attributes Inspector" earlier in this chapter to enter *mailto:* followed immediately by the e-mail address (see **Figure 36**).

or

Use PageMill to open a page containing the link you want to use and copy the link from there.

To add a link to a file

Follow the steps under "To add a link by typing in the Link Location Bar" or "To add a link by typing in the Attributes Inspector" earlier in this chapter to enter the complete URL of the file.

or

Use PageMill to open a page containing the link you want to use and copy the link from there.

About Image Maps

An image map lets you use one image to link to multiple destinations. You insert the image in a PageMill document, then create "hot spots" on the image, each of which is associated with a different address. PageMill automatically creates the HTML-encoded map files for you.

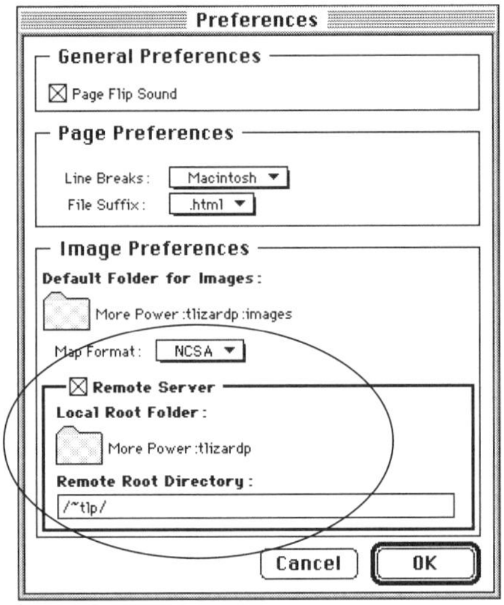

Figure 27. *Check the Map Format and Remote Server options before creating an image map.*

✔ Tip

- Before you create an image map, check the settings in the Preferences dialog box (see **Figure 27**) to be sure the correct settings are entered for the Map Format and Remote Server options. If these options are set incorrectly, your image map will not work. If you're not sure what to enter, ask your Webmaster or system administrator. I tell you about the Preferences dialog box in **Chapter 1**.

To open the image in Image view

In the PageMill window, double-click the image.

or

Choose Open from PageMill's File menu or press [⌘O] and use the Open dialog box that appears to locate and open the image.

The image opens in the Image view window (see **Figure 28**).

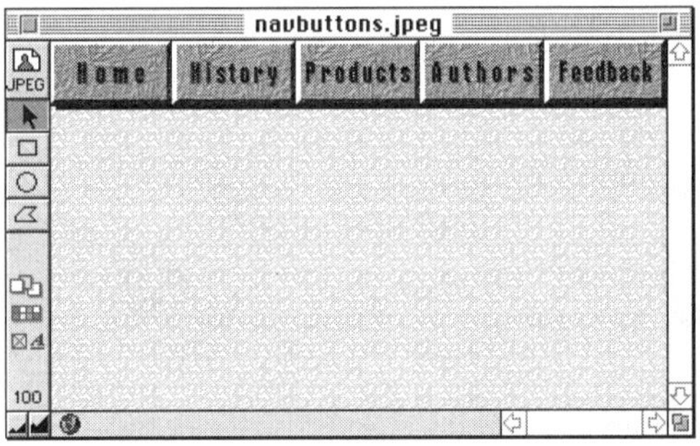

Figure 28. *You create image maps in Image view, using hot spot tools.*

✔ Tip

- I tell you more about Image view in **Chapter 5**.

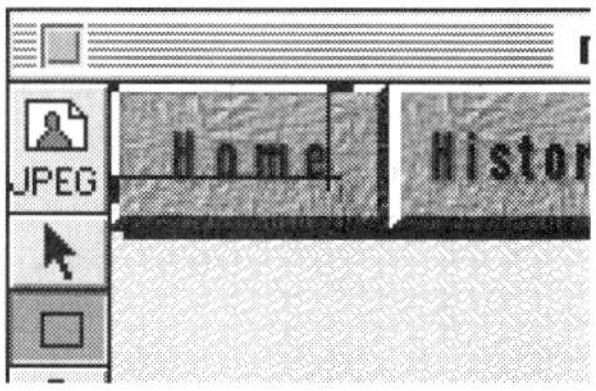

Figure 29. *To draw a rectangular or round hot spot, choose the appropriate tool and drag.*

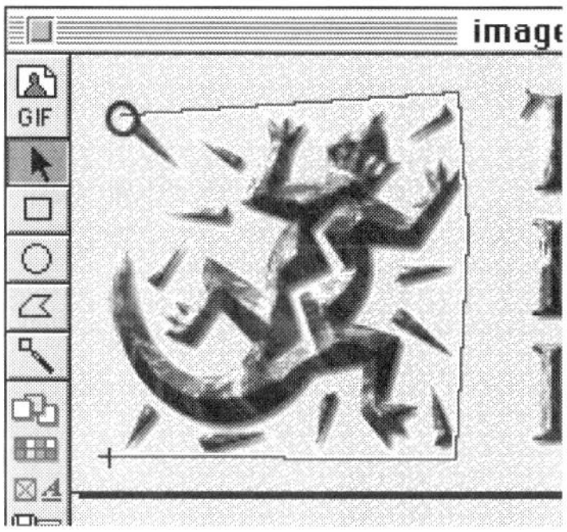

Figure 30. *To draw a polygon hot spot, choose the polygon tool and click to place corners.*

Figure 31. *Here's a completed rectangular hot spot. To resize it, drag a corner.*

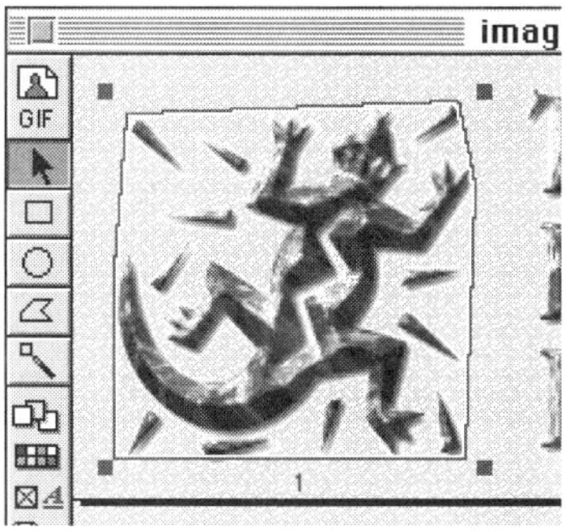

Figure 32. *Here's a completed polygon hot spot.*

- The number under each hot spot corresponds to its stacking order. If two or more spots overlap, the one with the lowest number is the one that will be activated when clicked.

To add hot spots to an image

1. Click the hot spot tool that most closely matches the shape of the hot spot you want to draw:
   - ▲ The rectangle hot spot tool draws rectangular or square hot spots. 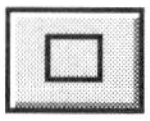
   - ▲ The circle hot spot tool draws round hot spots. 
   - ▲ The polygon hot spot tool draws multisided hot spots to your specifications. 
2. Move the mouse pointer, which should appear as a cross hair pointer, to the area where you want to draw a hot spot.
3. To use the rectangle or circle hot spot tool, drag to "draw" the shape (see **Figure 29**).

   or

   To use the polygon hot spot tool, click to position the corners of the polygon (see **Figure 30**), then click on the starting point to close the polygon.

   When you complete the shape, it appears in blue with resizing handles in its corners and a number beneath it (see **Figures 31** and **32**).

✔ Tips

- To draw a square hot spot, click the rectangle hot spot tool and hold down Shift while you drag.
- To change the size or shape of a hot spot, drag its resizing handles.
- To move a hot spot, position the mouse pointer in the middle of the hot spot, press the mouse button down, and drag to a new position.
- To delete a hot spot, click it to select it and press Delete or choose Clear from the Edit menu.

To add a link to a hot spot by dragging

To add a link to a page, drag the Page icon for the destination page onto the hot spot (see **Figure 33**).

or

To add a link to an anchor, drag the anchor icon for the destination onto the hot spot.

or

To add a link to an image, drag the image icon from an Image view window or from a Finder window onto the hot spot.

The name of the link appears in blue over the hot spot (see **Figure 34**).

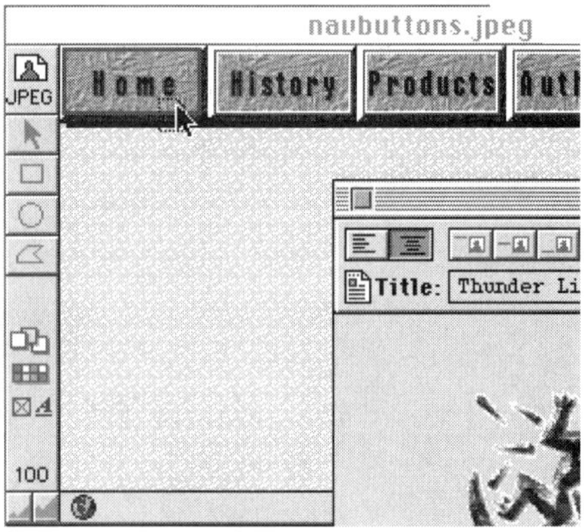

Figure 33. *One way to add a link to a hot spot is to drag a page icon onto it.*

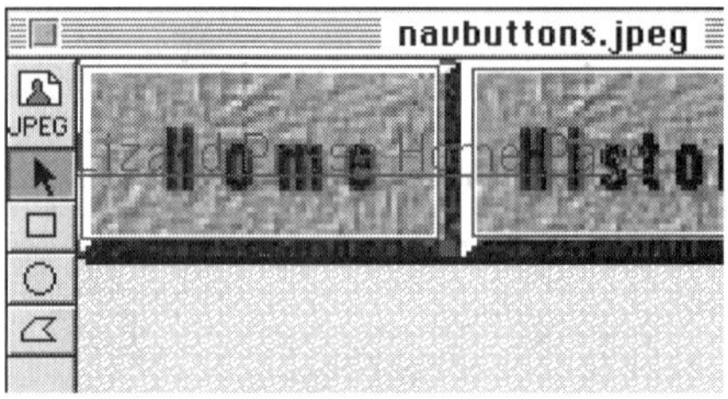

Figure 34. *The name of the link appears over the hot spot.*

To add a link to a hot spot by typing

1. Click the hot spot to select it.
2. Click in the Link Location Bar at the bottom of the window to activate it (see **Figure 35**).
3. Type the address for the destination (see **Figure 36**) and press Return or Enter to complete the entry.

The name of the link appears in blue over the hot spot.

Figure 35. *Another way to add a link is to select the hot spot, activate the Link Location Bar, …*

Figure 36. *…enter the address for the link, and press* Return.

To create a default link

1. Click on the image anywhere except on a hot spot so no hot spot is selected.
2. Click in the Link Location Bar at the bottom of the window to activate it (see **Figure 35**).
3. Type the address for the default destination and press Return or Enter to complete the entry.

The name of the link appears in blue in the lower left corner of the image (see **Figure 37**). This is the destination that will be displayed if someone clicks the image but misses the hot spots.

Figure 37. *When you add a default link, its name appears at the bottom left corner of the image.*

To remove a link from a hot spot

1. Click the hot spot containing the link to select it.
2. Click in the Link Location Bar at the bottom of the window to activate it, press Delete to delete its contents, and press Return or Enter to complete the entry.

The name of the link disappears from the hot spot.

Figure 38. *In this example, one hot spot (#1) is overlapping two others, making it impossible to click either of the two smaller spots.*

To change the stacking order of hot spots

1. Click the hot spot you want to change to select it (see **Figure 38**).
2. Click the layering tool to display a menu of four stacking options (see **Figure 39**):
   - ▲ Bring to Front assigns number 1 to the spot, thus putting it on the top of the stack.
   - ▲ Send to Back assigns the highest number to the spot, thus putting it on the bottom of the stack.
   - ▲ Shuffle Forward lowers the number of the spot by one, thus bringing it up one layer.
   - ▲ Shuffle Backward raises the number of the spot by one, thus sending it back one layer.

When you make your selection, the numbers under each of the hot spots change as necessary (see **Figure 40**).

Figure 39. *Use the Layering tool's pop-up menu to change the stacking order of overlapping hot spots.*

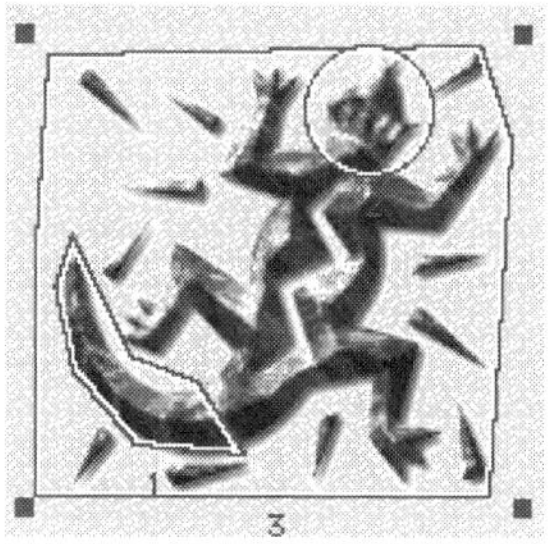

Figure 40. *By moving the large hot spot to the back, the other two spots are accessible. Note the way the numbers changed from* Figure 38.

✔ Tip

- ■ Stacking order is only important if the hot spots on an image map overlap.

Changing Hot Spot Stacking Order

To change hot spot color

1. Click the hot spot color icon to display a menu of fourteen colors (see **Figure 41**).
2. Choose a color that contrasts from the dominant color of the image.

The color changes for all hot spots and address text in the active Image view window. **Figures 42a** and **42b** illustrate the same image with the default hot spot color (see **Figure 42a**) and a bright yellow color (see **Figure 42b**).

✔ Tip

- Changing the hot spot color does not affect the way images that contain hot spots appear on Web pages since hot spot outlines are invisible.

To toggle hot spot label display

Click the Label Display switch.

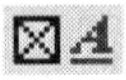

If you look closely, you'll see that the X in the switch's check box disappears when label display is turned off.

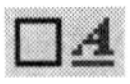

To change Image view magnification

To enlarge the view of the image (see **Figure 43**), click the large mountains on the magnification icon.

or

To reduce the view of the image (see **Figure 44**), click the small mountains on the magnification icon.

✔ Tips

- The zoom percentage is always indicated above the magnification icon (see **Figures 43** and **44**).
- Magnification percentages range from 12 to 800 percent.

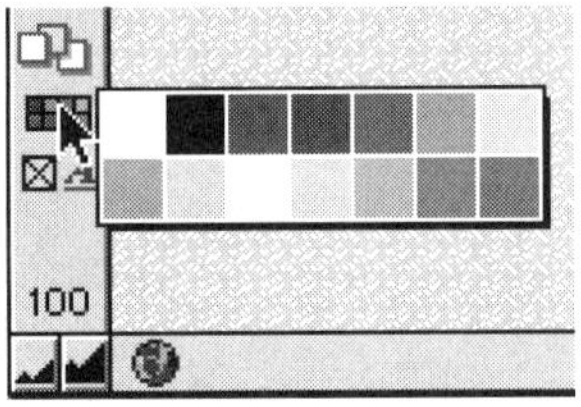

Figure 41. *Make hot spots more visible by changing their color.*

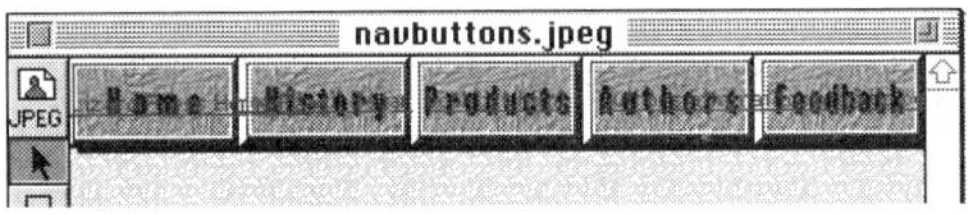

Figure 42a. *The hot spots and buttons are tough to see when their default blue color is against a dark background…*

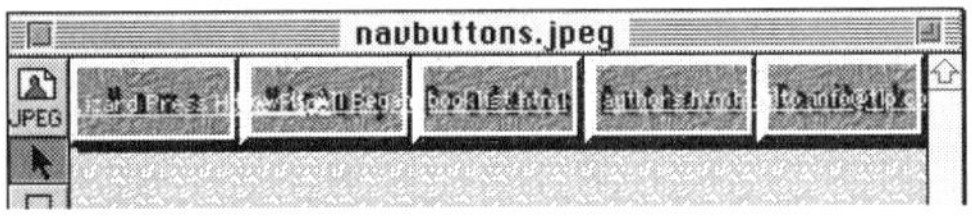

Figure 42b. *…but by changing the hot spot color to bright yellow, they really stand out.*

Figure 43. *Click the large mountains to zoom in…*

Figure 44. *…or click the small mountains to zoom out.*

Figure 45. *Use the Save command to save the hot spots and links you add to an image.*

To save image map hot spots and links

Choose Save from the File menu (see **Figure 45**).

or

Press ⌘S.

✔ Tip

- When you save an image containing hot spots and links, PageMill automatically creates an image map file for it. How the file is named depends on the Map Format selected in the Preferences dialog box (see **Figure 27**).

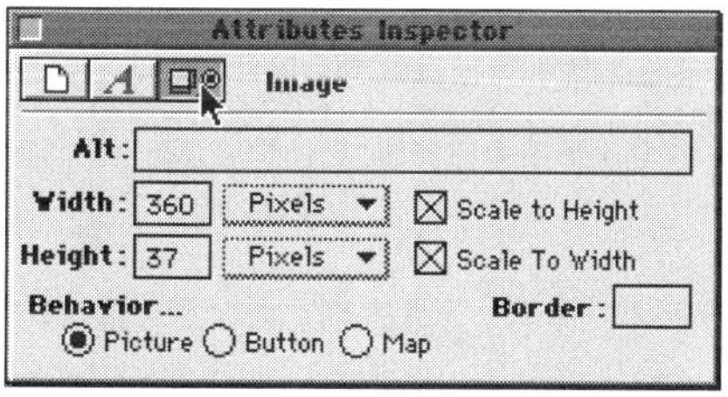

Figure 46. *Click the Objects button in the Attributes Inspector to view the Image options.*

Figure 47. *Turn on the Map radio button.*

To set an image as a map

1. If necessary, save the image and close the Image view window for the image.
2. In the PageMill window, click the image to select it.
3. Choose Show Attributes Inspector from the Window menu or press ⌘; to display the Attributes Inspector.
4. Click the Object button on the Attributes Inspector's button bar to display Image options (see **Figure 46**).
5. Click the Map radio button to select it (see **Figure 47**).

✔ Tip

- If you fail to set an image containing hot spots as a map, the hot spots won't work.

To set the image map location

1. In the PageMill window, click the image to select it.
2. Choose Show Attributes Inspector from the Window menu or press ⌘; to display the Attributes Inspector.
3. Click the Text button on the Attributes Inspector's button bar to display Text options (see **Figure 48**).
4. Click inside the Location edit box to activate it.
5. Type the pathname for the image map and press Return or Enter to complete the entry.

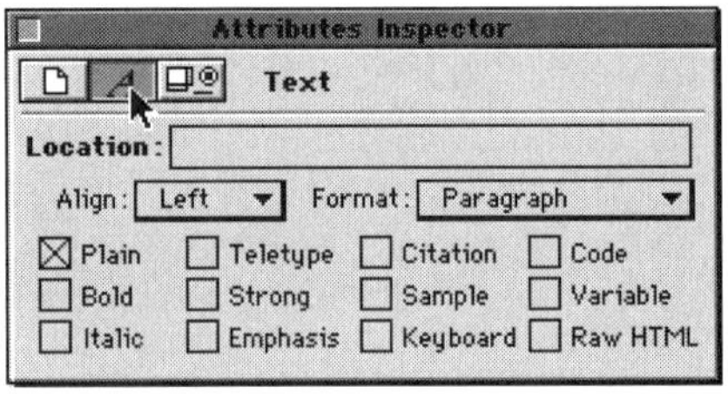

Figure 48. *You tell the server where to find the map by entering it in the Location edit box of the Attributes Inspector.*

✔ Tips

- The pathname entry varies depending on the Web server software. For example, some servers require both a CGI script name and the name of the map. Other servers require only a partial pathname for the map.
- If you're not sure what to enter as a pathname for the map, check with your Webmaster or system administrator. Or find another image map that works and look at its Location setting.
- If you do not set the correct path in the location window, the image map will not work.
- If you prefer, you can click the image to select it, then activate the Link Location Bar at the bottom of the screen and type the path for the map location there. Don't forget to press Return or Enter to complete the entry.

CREATING FORMS 7

About Forms

Forms are Web pages with special elements designed to gather information. You create a form by adding any combination of the following form elements to a Web page:

Figure 1. *Here's a form that combines many form elements.*

- *Check boxes,* which can be used to select multiple items from a list.
- *Radio buttons,* which let users choose from a variety of options.
- *Text areas,* which accept long passages of text.
- *Text fields,* which accept short strings of text.
- *Password fields,* which let users enter passwords.
- *Pop up menus* and *selection list fields,* which let users choose from a variety of options.
- *Submit button,* which sends data on completed forms to be processed.
- *Reset button,* which clears all entries so the user can start over.

Figure 1 shows an example that uses almost all of these elements.

✔ Tip

- In order to use a form, you need a program called a CGI. I tell you more about CGIs at the end of this chapter.

About Creating Forms

With PageMill, you create forms by placing form elements, text, and images on a page.

- Form elements (see **Figure 2**) collect input from the user. Each one must have a unique name and/or value that is recognized by the CGI with which the form will be used.
- Text labels or descriptions (see **Figure 3**) identify the kind of information requested by each form element. Text can be formatted as desired. I tell you about entering and formatting text in **Chapters 2**, **3**, and **4**.
- Images (see **Figure 4**) and graphic elements like horizontal rules add visual appeal to your forms. I tell you about working with graphic images in **Chapter 5**.

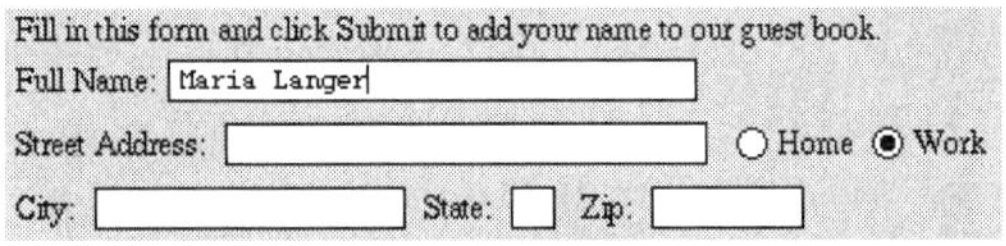

Figure 2. *Form elements like the text fields and radio buttons shown here gather information.*

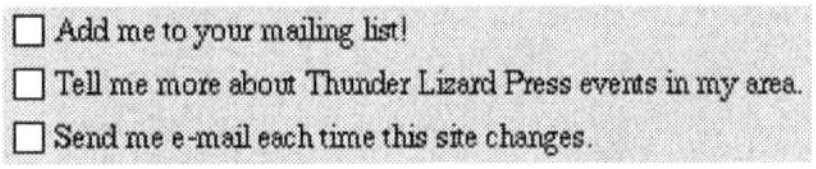

Figure 3. *Without text labels beside each of these check boxes, how would the user know what to check?*

Figure 4. *Images and graphic elements make forms more visually appealing.*

✔ Tips

- PageMill supports only one form per page.
- You can copy form elements within a form or from one form to another using the Copy and Paste commands or by holding down Option while dragging a selected element. I discuss copying techniques in **Chapter 2**.
- To delete a form element, simply select it and press Delete or choose Clear from the Edit menu.
- Once you create a form, its structure isn't set in stone. You can reorganize it any way you like. Use the basic text and image entry, formatting, and editing techniques discussed in **Chapters 2** through **5** to change your forms as needed.

About Check Boxes

Check boxes are used when you want to provide a list and let the user select more than one option. Unlike radio buttons, which I discuss later in this chapter, a user can turn on any number of check boxes in a group.

To add a check box

1. Position the insertion point where you want the check box to appear (see **Figure 5**).
2. Click the Insert Checkbox button. 

   or

   Press ⌘ Control 3.

   A check box appears at the insertion point (see **Figure 6**).
3. Type in a label or descriptive text for the check box.
4. Repeat steps 1 through 3 for each check box you want to add.

When you're finished, your check boxes might look something like the ones in **Figure 7**.

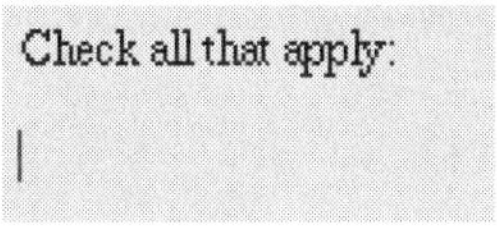

Figure 5. *Position the insertion point where you want the check box to appear.*

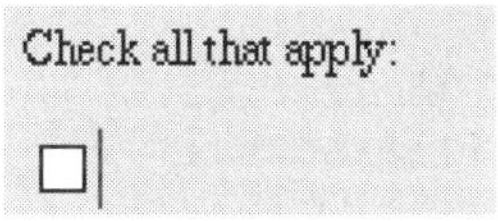

Figure 6. *The check box appears at the insertion point.*

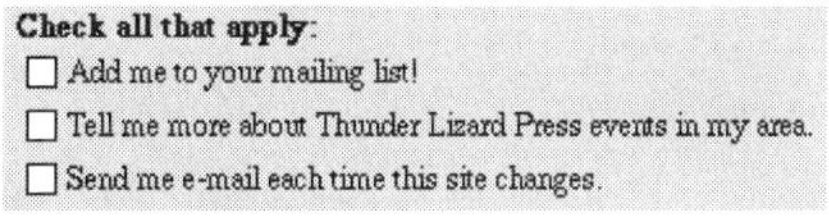

Figure 7. *Finished check boxes.*

✔ Tip

- If you want to set up your check boxes in multiple columns, use the Preformatted paragraph format to set up a table with columns that are padded with spaces (see **Figure 8**). I tell you about the Preformatted format in **Chapter 4**.

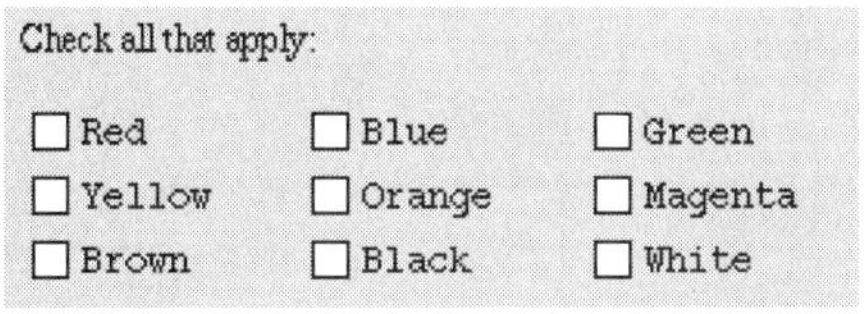

Figure 8. *Use the Preformatted format to arrange check boxes in columns.*

To specify check box settings

1. Select the check box for which you want to specify settings (see **Figure 9**).
2. Choose Show Attributes Inspector from the Window menu (see **Figure 10**).

   or

   Press [⌘][;].
3. Click the Object button in the Attributes Inspector window that appears (see **Figure 11**) to view the Checkbox options.
4. Click in the Name edit box to activate it and type in a name. Press [Return] or [Enter] to complete the entry.
5. Click in the Value edit box to activate it and type in a value (see **Figure 12**). Press [Return] or [Enter] to complete the entry.
6. To set the check box so it is turned on by default, turn on the Checked check box.

✔ Tips

- The Name and Value you assign to a check box must meet the requirements of the CGI that will process the form. Consult the CGI documentation for specifics.
- You must press [Return] or [Enter] to complete any entry you make in an edit box within the Attributes Inspector.

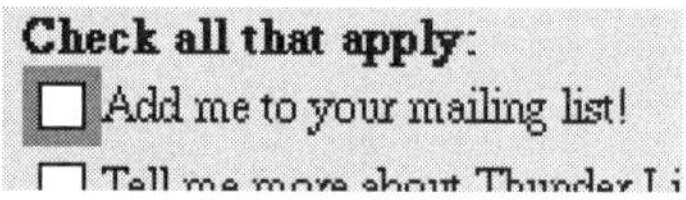

Figure 9. *Click a check box to select it.*

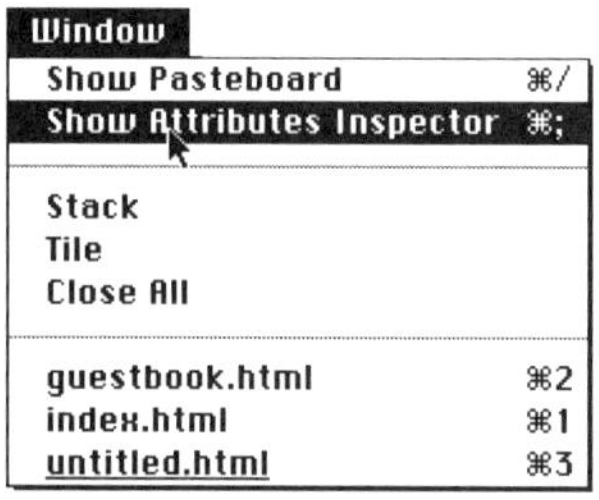

Figure 10. *Choose Show Attributes Inspector from the Window menu to display the Attributes Inspector.*

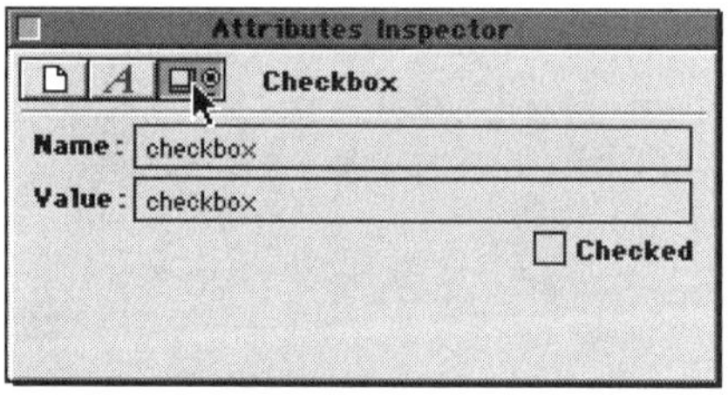

Figure 11. *The Attributes Inspector's Checkbox options.*

Figure 12. *Enter a Value in the Value edit box and press* [Return].

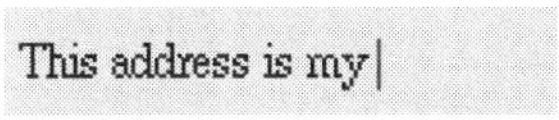

Figure 13. *Position the insertion point where you want the first radio button to appear.*

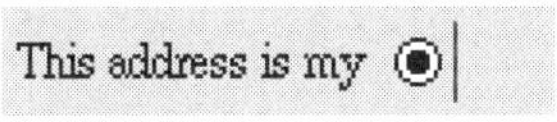

Figure 14. *The radio button appears at the insertion point.*

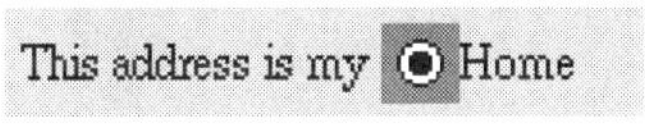

Figure 15. *Select the first radio button.*

Figure 16. *Clone or copy it to create a second radio button in the group.*

Figure 17. *When you're finished making radio buttons for a group, only one will be selected.*

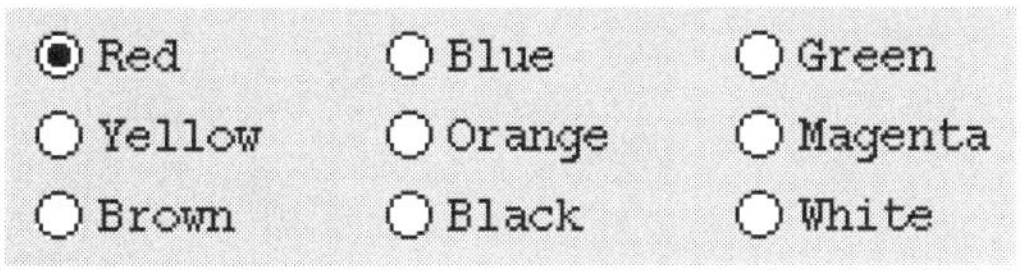

Figure 18. *Use the Preformatted format to arrange radio buttons in columns.*

✔ Tips

- You must copy or clone radio buttons to create a group. If you use the Insert Radio Button button for each one, they will not be part of the same group.
- If you want to set up your radio buttons in multiple columns, use the Preformatted paragraph format to set up a table with columns that are padded with spaces (see **Figure 18**). I tell you about the Preformatted format in **Chapter 4**.

About Radio Buttons

Radio buttons are used when you want to provide a list and let the user select exactly one option. Unlike check boxes, which I discuss on the previous pages, a user must select one—and only one—radio button in a group.

To add a group of radio buttons

1. Position the insertion point where you want the first radio button to appear (see **Figure 13**).
2. Click the Insert Radio Button button.

   or

   Press [⌘] [Control] [4].

   A radio button appears at the insertion point (see **Figure 14**).
3. Type in a label or descriptive text for the radio button.
4. Click the radio button to select it (see **Figure 15**).
5. Use the Copy and Paste commands to place a copy of the button where you want another radio button to appear.

   or

   Hold down [Option] and drag the first radio button to where you want another radio button to appear.

   A radio button appears where you pasted or Option-dragged the first radio button (see **Figure 16**). Note that only one of the radio buttons is turned on.
6. Type in a label or descriptive text for the new radio button.
7. Repeat steps 4 through 6 for each radio button you want to add to the group.

When you're finished, your radio buttons might look something like the ones in **Figure 17**.

To specify radio button settings

1. Select the radio button for which you want to specify settings (see **Figure 15**).
2. Choose Show Attributes Inspector from the Window menu (see **Figure 10**).

   or

   Press [⌘] [;].
3. Click the Object button in the Attributes Inspector window that appears (see **Figure 19**) to view the Radio button options.
4. Click in the Name edit box to activate it and type in a name. Press [Return] or [Enter] to complete the entry.
5. Click in the Value edit box to activate it and type in a value (see **Figure 20**). Press [Return] or [Enter] to complete the entry.
6. To set the radio button so it is the one that is selected by default, turn on the Checked check box.

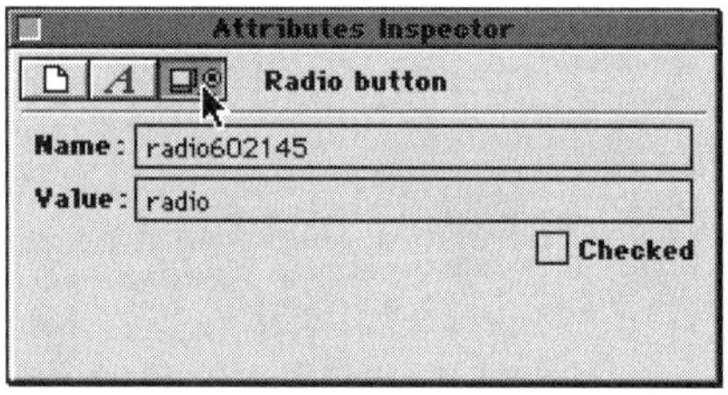

Figure 19. *The Attributes Inspector's Radio button options.*

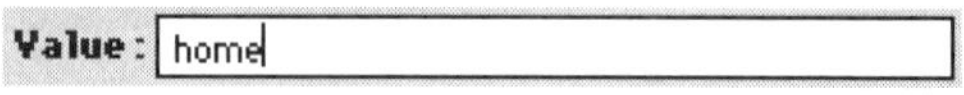

Figure 20. *Enter a value in the Value edit box and press* [Return].

✔ Tips

- The Name and Value you assign to a radio button must meet the requirements of the CGI that will process the form. Consult the CGI documentation for specifics.
- All radio buttons in a group have the same name. If you change the name of one radio button in a group, be sure to change the names of the others so they match.
- To make radio buttons inserted separately into a group of radio buttons, change their names so they're all the same.
- You must press [Return] or [Enter] to complete any entry you make in an edit box within the Attributes Inspector.

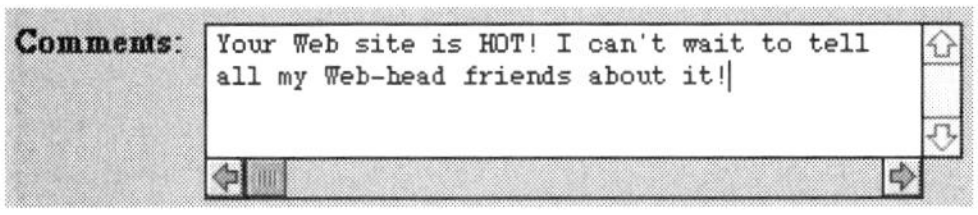

Figure 21. *A text area accepts multiple-line text entries.*

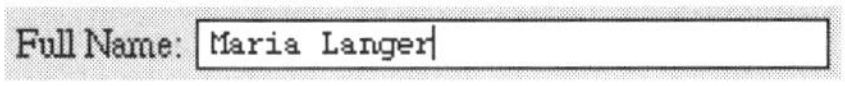

Figure 22. *A text field accepts only one line of text.*

Figure 23. *A password field echoes its contents with bullets or asterisks.*

Figure 24. *Position the insertion point where you want the element to appear.*

Figure 25. *The element you chose appears at the insertion point.*

About Text Input Elements

Text input form elements collect typed input from users. There are three kinds of text elements:

- A text area (see **Figure 21**) accepts multiple-line text entries. It is designed for lengthy input.
- A text field (see **Figure 22**) accepts a single line of text. It is designed for short input.
- A password field (see **Figure 23**) accepts a single line of text. It is specially designed for password entry since input is echoed back as bullet or asterisk characters.

To add a text input element

1. Position the insertion point where you want the element to appear. In most cases, this will be right after or under a typed-in label or descriptive text (see **Figure 24**).
2. Click one of the following button bar buttons or press one of the following Command key equivalents:
   - ▲ To insert a text area, click the Insert Text Area button or press ⌘ Control 5. 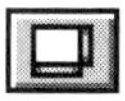
   - ▲ To insert a text field, click the Insert Text Field button or press ⌘ Control 6. 
   - ▲ To insert a password field, click the Insert Password Field button or press ⌘ Control 7. 

   The element you inserted appears at the insertion point (see **Figure 25**).
3. Repeat steps 1 and 2 for each input element you want to add.

To resize a text area by dragging

1. Click on the text area to select it.

   A selection box and three resizing handles appear around it (see **Figure 26**).

2. Position the mouse pointer on one of the resizing handles, press the mouse button down, and drag.

   ▲ To change the width of the text area, drag the right side resizing handle.

   ▲ To change the height of the text area, drag the bottom resizing handle.

   ▲ To change the width and height of the text area, drag the corner resizing handle.

   As you drag, an outline of the text area appears to indicate the final size (see **Figure 27**).

3. When the text area is the desired size, release the mouse button.

   The text area resizes to your specifications (see **Figure 28**).

Figure 26. *Click a text area to select it.*

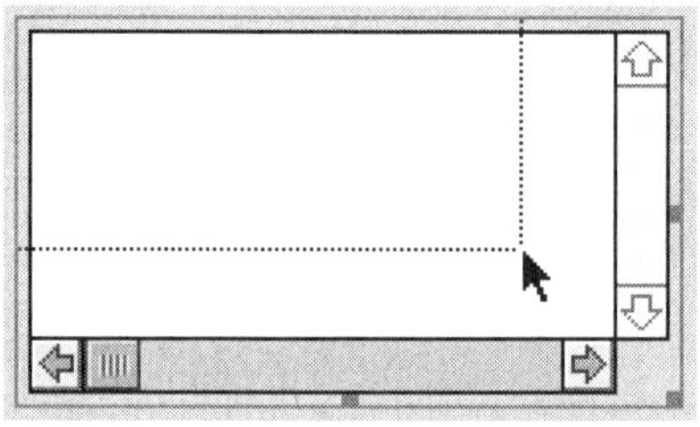

Figure 27. *Drag one of its resizing handles to make it bigger or smaller.*

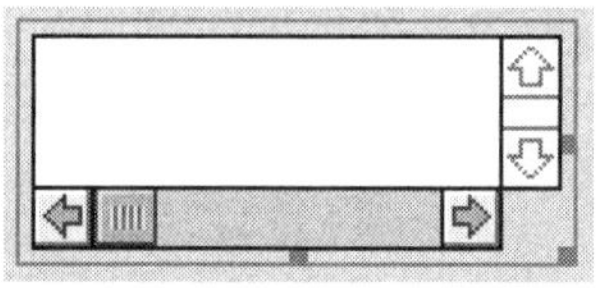

Figure 28. *When you release the mouse button, the size changes.*

To resize a text field or password field by dragging

1. Click on the text field or password field to select it.

   A selection box appears around it and one resizing handle appears on its right side (see **Figure 29**).

2. Position the mouse pointer on the resizing handle, press the mouse button down, and drag to the left or right.

   As you drag, an outline of the field appears to indicate the final size (see **Figure 30**).

3. When the field is the desired size, release the mouse button.

   The field resizes to your specifications (see **Figure 31**).

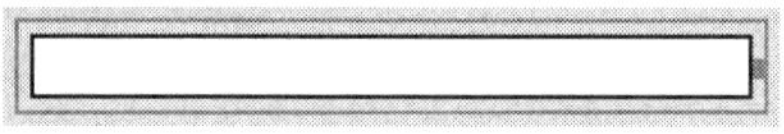

Figure 29. *Click a text or password field to select it.*

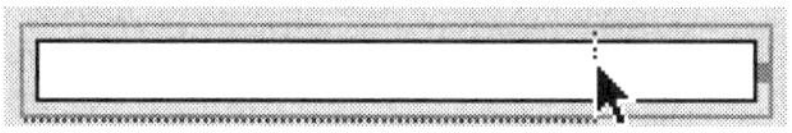

Figure 30. *Drag its resizing handle to make it longer or shorter.*

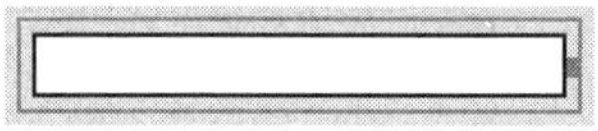

Figure 31. *When you release the mouse button, the size changes.*

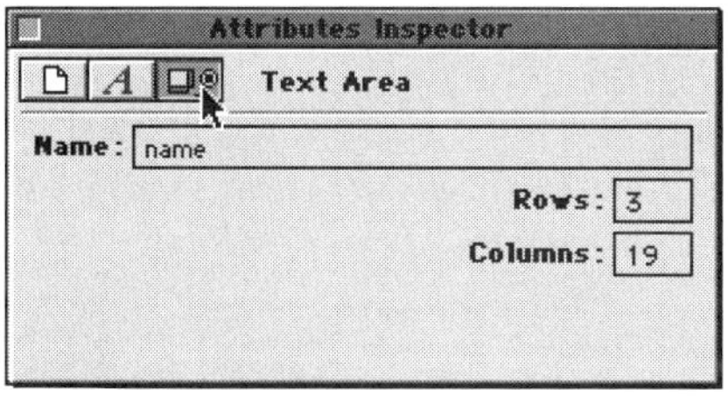

Figure 32. *The Attributes Inspectors Text Area options, ...*

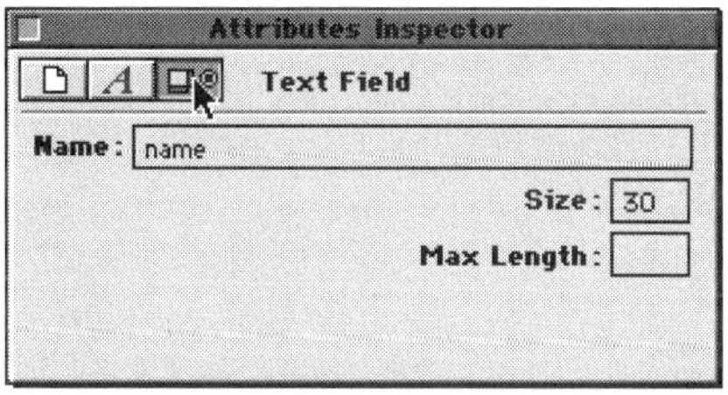

Figure 33. *...Text Field options, ...*

Figure 34. *... and Password Field options are all very similar.*

Figure 35. *Enter a new value in the Size edit box to change field size.*

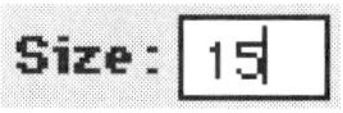

To resize a text input element with the Attributes Inspector

1. Click on the text area, text field, or password field to select it.
2. Choose Show Attributes Inspector from the Window menu (see **Figure 10**).

   or

   Press [⌘][;].
3. Click the Object button in the Attributes Inspector window that appears to view the Text Area (see **Figure 32**), Text Field (see **Figure 33**), or Password Field (see **Figure 34**) options.
4. Click in the Size, Max Length, Rows, or Columns edit box to activate it and enter a new value (see **Figure 35**). Press [Return] or [Enter] to complete the entry. Do this for each value you want to change.

✔ Tips

- All sizes are expressed in terms of characters.
- When you make a change to one of the size-related values in the Attributes Inspector, the size of the select input element changes accordingly. The same holds true when you change the size of an element by dragging it—the values in the Attributes Inspector change accordingly.
- If you specify a Max Length value for a Text Field or Password Field, the field will not get any larger than the number of characters you specify.
- You must press [Return] or [Enter] to complete any entry you make in an edit box within the Attributes Inspector.

To specify a default value for a text input element

1. Double-click the element for which you want to specify a default value.

   A dark border appears around it and an insertion point appears inside it (see **Figure 36**).
2. Enter the value you want to appear (see **Figure 37**).

Figure 36. *Double-click the element in which you want to enter a default value.*

Figure 37. *Enter the value you want to use as a default.*

✔ Tip

- Default text can be used when a field has a common response or when you want to provide hints on how text should be entered (see **Figure 37**).

To name a text input element

1. Select the text input element you want to name (see **Figure 38**).
2. Choose Show Attributes Inspector from the Window menu (see **Figure 10**).

   or

   Press ⌘;.
3. Click the Object button in the Attributes Inspector window that appears to view the Text Area, Text Field (see **Figure 39**), or Password Field options.
4. Click in the Name edit box to activate it and type in a name (see **Figure 40**). Press Return or Enter to complete the entry.

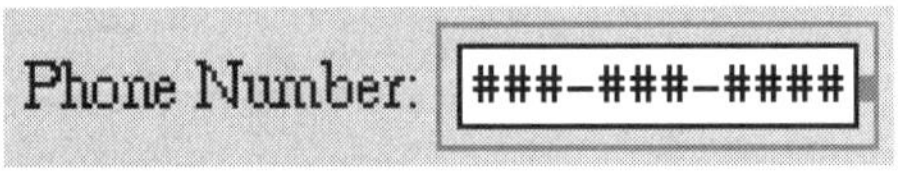

Figure 38. *Click the element to select it.*

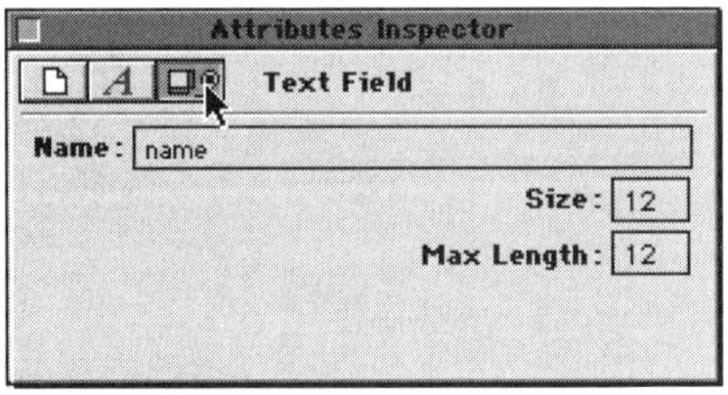

Figure 39. *The Attributes Inspector's Text Field options.*

Figure 40. *Enter a name in the Name edit box and press* Return.

✔ Tips

- The Name you assign to a text input area must meet the requirements of the CGI that will process the form. Consult the CGI documentation for specifics.
- You must press Return or Enter to complete any entry you make in an edit box within the Attributes Inspector.

About Pop-up Menus

A pop-up menu enables the user to choose one option from a menu you provide.

✔ Tip

- Pop-up menus can be converted to list selection fields. I tell you about list selection fields later in this chapter.

Figure 41. *Position the insertion point where you want the pop-up menu to appear.*

Figure 42. *A pop-up menu with PageMill's default values appears.*

To add a pop-up menu

1. Position the insertion point where you want the pop-up menu to appear. In most cases, this will be right after or under a typed-in label or descriptive text (see **Figure 41**).
2. Click the Insert Popup button. 

   or

   Press ⌘ Control 8.

   The pop-up menu appears at the insertion point (see **Figure 42**).

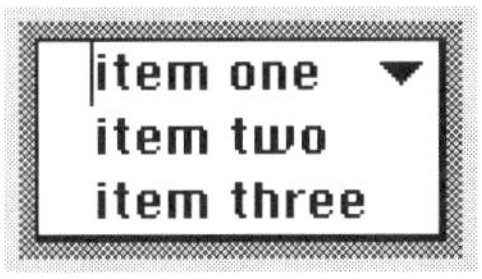

Figure 43. *Double-click a pop-up menu to edit it.*

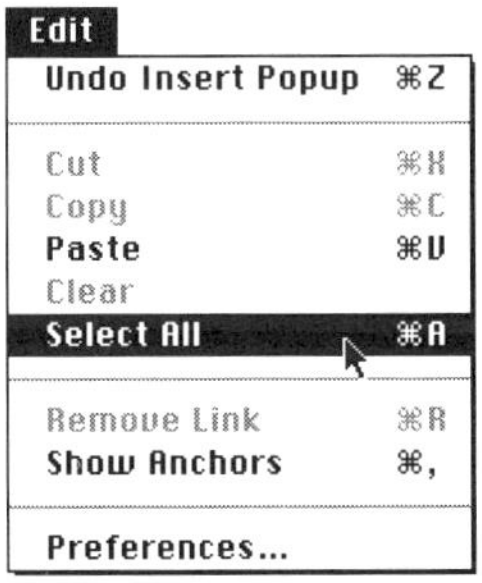

Figure 44. *Choose Select All from the Edit menu to select all the options in the list.*

Figure 45. *Enter the options you want to appear on the menu.*

To specify pop-up menu options

1. Double-click the pop-up menu for which you want to specify options.

   The list opens to display the default options (see **Figure 43**).
2. Select all the default options by dragging the mouse over them, choosing Select All from the Edit menu (see **Figure 44**), or pressing ⌘ A.
3. Type in the values you want. Be sure to press Return after each one.

   When you're finished, your list might look like the one in **Figure 45**.
4. Click elsewhere in the page window to close the menu options window.

✔ Tip

- You can also use this technique to edit the values in a pop-up menu if you need to change them.

To set a default menu option

1. Double-click the pop-up menu for which you want to set a default option.

   The list opens to display the options (see **Figure 45**).
2. Drag the triangle into position beside the value you want to set as the default (see **Figure 46**).
3. Click elsewhere in the page window to close the menu options window.

The entry you set as the default appears on the menu (see **Figure 47**).

✔ Tip

- Although you can use this technique to set any option as the default, the default value in a pop-up menu is usually the first one on the menu.

To name a pop-up menu

1. Select the pop-up menu you want to name (see **Figure 48**).
2. Choose Show Attributes Inspector from the Window menu (see **Figure 10**).

   or

   Press [⌘] [;].
3. Click the Object button in the Attributes Inspector window that appears to view the Selection Field options (see **Figure 49**).
4. Click in the Name edit box to activate it and type in a name (see **Figure 50**). Press [Return] or [Enter] to complete the entry.

Figure 46. *Drag the arrow into position beside the default value on the menu.*

Figure 47. *The option with the arrow beside it is the one that appears when the menu is closed.*

Figure 48. *Click the pop-up menu to select it.*

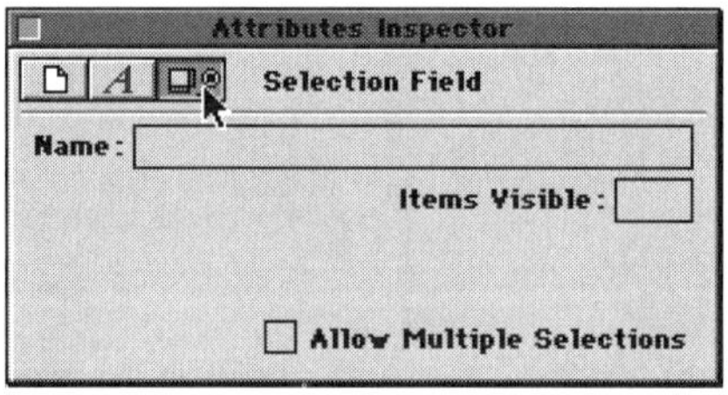

Figure 49. *The Attributes Inspector's Selection Field options.*

Figure 50. *Type a new name in the Name edit box and press [Return].*

✔ Tips

- The Name you assign to a pop-up menu must meet the requirements of the CGI that will process the form. Consult the CGI documentation for specifics.
- You must press [Return] or [Enter] to complete any entry you make in an edit box within the Attributes Inspector.

About List Selection Fields

A list selection field lets users select one or more options from a scrolling list. List selection fields are created by setting options in the Attributes Inspector for a pop-up menu.

To add a list selection field

1. Follow the steps in the "To add a pop-up menu" and "To specify pop-up menu options" sections to add a pop-up menu and specify menu options.
2. Select the pop-up menu you created (see **Figure 48**).
3. Choose Show Attributes Inspector from the Window menu (see **Figure 10**).

   or

   Press ⌘ ;.
4. Click the Object button in the Attributes Inspector window that appears to view the Selection Field options (see **Figure 49**).
5. Click in the Items Visible edit box to activate it and type in the number of menu items you want to appear in the scrolling list (see **Figure 51**). Press Return or Enter to complete the entry.

   The pop-up list expands to show the number of items you specified. A scroll bar appears on the right side of the box (see **Figure 52**). It will now function as a scrolling list.

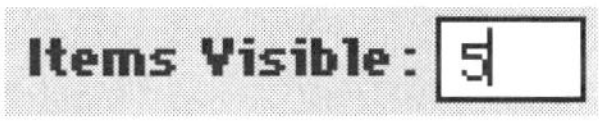

Figure 51. *Enter a value greater than 1 in the Items Visible edit box and press* Return.

Figure 52. *The number of options you specified appears in a scrolling list.*

Figure 53. *Or drag the handle at the bottom of a pop-up menu...*

Figure 54. *...to turn it into a scrolling list.*

✔ Tips

- To allow more than one selection from the list selection field, turn on the Allow Multiple Selections check box in the Attributes Inspector (see **Figure 49**).
- Another way to turn a pop-up list into a list selection field is to select it and drag its bottom resizing handle (see **Figures 53** and **54**).

About Submit & Reset Buttons

Forms usually include two special buttons:

- The Submit button sends the information from the form to the CGI on the server.
- The Reset button clears all entries in the form so the user can start fresh.

To add a Submit or Reset button

1. Position the insertion point where you want the button to appear.
2. Click one of the following buttons or press one of the following Command key equivalents:
   - ▲ To add a Submit button, click the Insert Submit Button button or press ⌘ Control 9.

   - ▲ To add a Reset button, click the Insert Reset Button button or press ⌘ Control 0.

The button you inserted appears at the insertion point (see **Figure 55**).

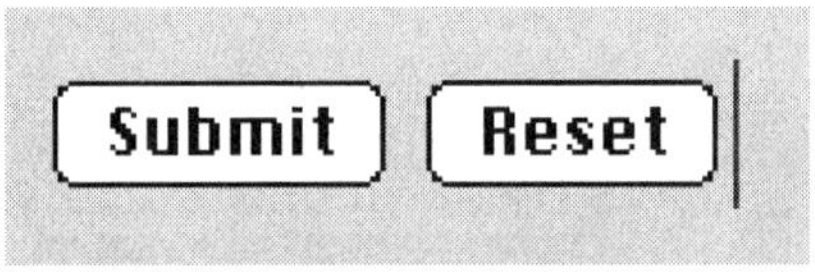

Figure 55. *The Submit and Reset buttons, which are standard equipment for forms, are normally placed together.*

✔ Tips

- You should only have one Submit button on a form.
- Submit and Reset buttons are normally placed together on a form.
- In most cases, Submit and Reset buttons are placed at the bottom of a form, right after the last input area.

To change the name of a button

1. Double-click the button.

   A dark border appears around it and an insertion point appears inside it (see **Figure 56**).
2. Edit the name of the button by selecting it and typing your changes (see **Figure 57**). The button resizes to accommodate the text inside it.
3. Click elsewhere in the page window to accept your changes.

Figure 56. *Double-click a button to edit it.*

Figure 57. *As you enter new text to appear on the button, the button resizes to accommodate it.*

To use an image as a Submit button

1. Select the image you want to use as a Submit button (see **Figure 58**).
2. Choose Show Attributes Inspector from the Window menu (see **Figure 10**).

   or

   Press ⌘;.
3. Click the Object button in the Attributes Inspector window that appears to view the Image options (see **Figure 59**).
4. Select the Button radio button under Behavior (see **Figure 60**).

A blue border appears around the image to indicate that it is a button (see **Figure 61**).

Figure 58. *Click the image you want to turn into a button to select it.*

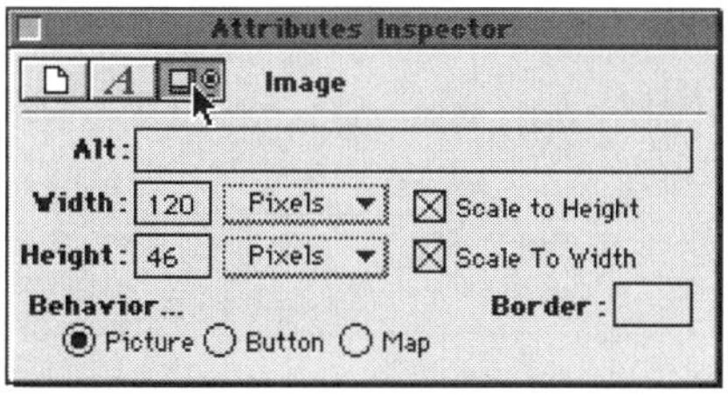

Figure 59. *The Attributes Inspector's Image options.*

Figure 60. *Select the Button radio button.*

Figure 61. *A blue border around the image indicates that it's a button.*

About CGIs

Forms work with programs called CGIs (Common Gateway Interfaces) that run on the Web server. When a user fills in a form and clicks the Submit button, the information gathered by the form is processed by the CGI. The CGI can do almost anything with the data, like:

- Send the data to someone via e-mail.
- Add the data to a database maintained in another application.
- Use the data to form the basis of a database search, perform the search, and display the results.
- Use the data to create a Web page.

✔ Tips

- The CGI's functionality (not the form itself) determines how the data is used.
- If you do not have a CGI to process data collected with a form, the form is useless.
- CGIs can be created with AppleScript (on Apple Servers) or other programming languages or purchased from third party vendors.

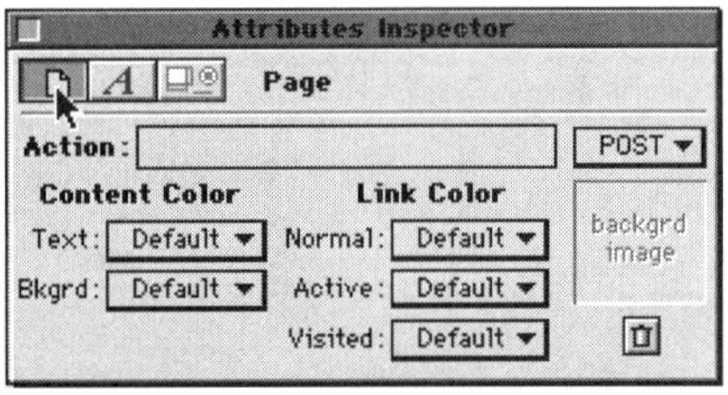

Figure 62. *The Attributes Inspector's Page options.*

To specify a CGI for a form

1. Choose Show Attributes Inspector from the Window menu (see **Figure 10**).

   or

   Press [⌘][;].
2. Click the Page button in the Attributes Inspector window that appears to view the Page options (see **Figure 62**).
3. Click in the Action edit box to activate it and type in the pathname for the CGI. Press [Return] or [Enter] to complete the entry.
4. Choose Get or Post from the pop-up menu beside the Action edit box (see **Figure 63**).

Figure 63. *If necessary, change the option selected on the menu beside the Action edit box.*

✔ Tip

- If you're not sure what to enter in the Action edit box or choose from the pop-up menu beside it, ask your Webmaster or system administrator.

SETTING PAGE ATTRIBUTES 8

About Page Attributes

PageMill makes it easy to set options that affect the entire page, like:

- Page Title, which appears in the title bar of a Web browser when the page is viewed.
- Background image, which puts a texture or image behind page text.
- Background color, which changes the color behind page text.
- Text color, which changes the color of text on a page.
- Link colors, which change the color of unvisited, visited, and active links on a page.

Most of these changes are made with the Attributes Inspector.

✔ Tip

- Although it isn't necessary to set any of these options for your pages, by changing the default values on each page, you can add visual appeal and give your pages a consistent look and feel that set them apart from other pages on the Web.

About the Page Title

The page title is the name of the page as it appears on the World Wide Web. When you specify a page name, that name appears in the title bar of Web browser windows (see **Figure 1**).

Figure 1. *When you give your page a title, that title appears in the title bar of Web browsers like Netscape Navigator.*

✔ Tips

- The page title is not the same as the page name. The page name, which you specify when you save a file, is subject to file naming restrictions based on your Web server. The page title, however, can be almost anything you like. I tell you about saving files in **Chapter 2**.
- A page title is used as a link name if you create a link by dragging a Page icon into another page window. I tell you about creating links in **Chapter 6**.

To add a page title

1. Click in the Title edit box near the top of the page window to activate it (see **Figure 2**).
2. Type the title you want to assign.
3. Press Return or Enter to complete the entry.

The title you entered appears in the Title edit box (see **Figure 3**).

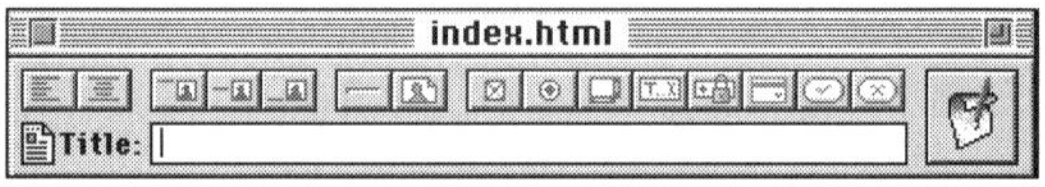

Figure 2. *Activate the Title edit box.*

Figure 3. *When you enter a title and press* Return, *the title appears in the title box.*

To edit or remove a page title

1. Click in the Title edit box to activate it.
2. Make changes as desired to edit the title.

   or

   Select the title and press Delete to delete it.
3. Press Return or Enter to complete the entry.

Your change is reflected in the Title edit box.

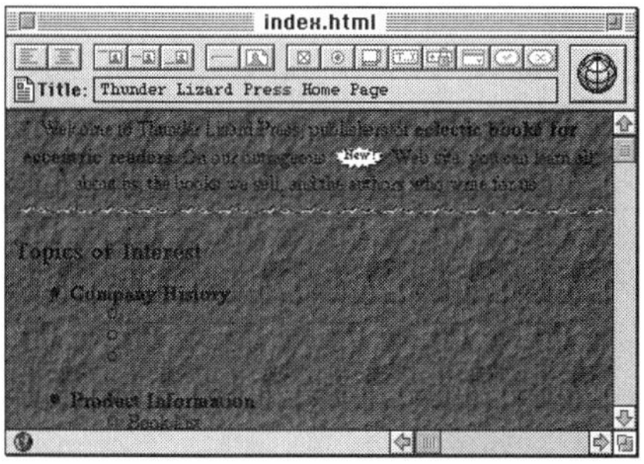

Figure 4. *Default colored text disappears against a dark background…*

Figure 5. *…or a busy background.*

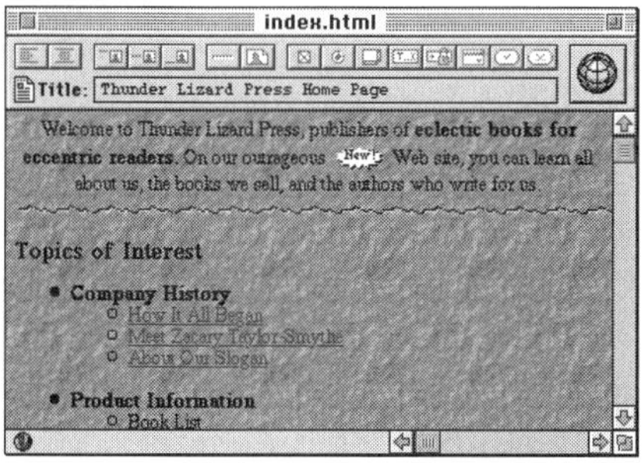

Figure 6. *By lightening and reducing contrast, the text shows through…*

Figure 7. *…even on busy backgrounds.*

About Background Images

A background image is an image that is used as a background pattern or texture behind the text and other images on a Web page. A background image can add a professional polish to a Web page.

✔ Tips

- For best results, use small background images. They take less time to load so your pages display more quickly.
- You can speed up page loading by using a limited number of background images on the Web pages at your site. Since Web browsers cache recently downloaded page and image files, they don't need to download the same files repeatedly during the session.
- Be sure the color of a background image contrasts with the color of page text. If the colors are too similar, page text will be illegible (see **Figure 4**). To remedy this problem, either change the color of the background image or the text. I tell you how to change text color later in this chapter.
- Try not to use "busy" images for backgrounds. Images with too many rich colors make poor backgrounds because text and other images on top of them are difficult to see clearly (see **Figure 5**).
- You can make an otherwise unsuitable image more appropriate for use as a background pattern by lightening it and reducing its contrast in a graphics application like Photoshop (see **Figures 6** and **7**).
- You can use the Transparency tool in the Image view window to make the background of an image transparent before using it as a background image. I tell you how to work with Image view in **Chapter 5**.

To add a background image with the Attributes Inspector

1. Choose Show Attributes Inspector from the Window menu or press ⌘;.
2. Click the Page button to display the Attributes Inspector's Page options (see **Figure 8**).
3. With the PageMill application active, drag a GIF or JPEG image file icon from the Finder to the Backgrd Image area on the Attributes Inspector (see **Figure 9**).

   or

   Drag an image from the PageMill window to the Backgrd Image area on the Attributes Inspector (see **Figure 10**).

When you release the mouse button, the image fills the Backgrd Image area in the Attributes Inspector and becomes a repeating pattern in the background of the page (see **Figure 11**).

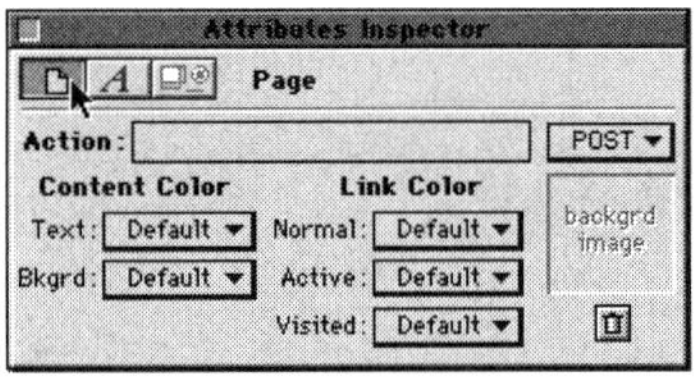

Figure 8. *The Page options of the Attributes Inspector.*

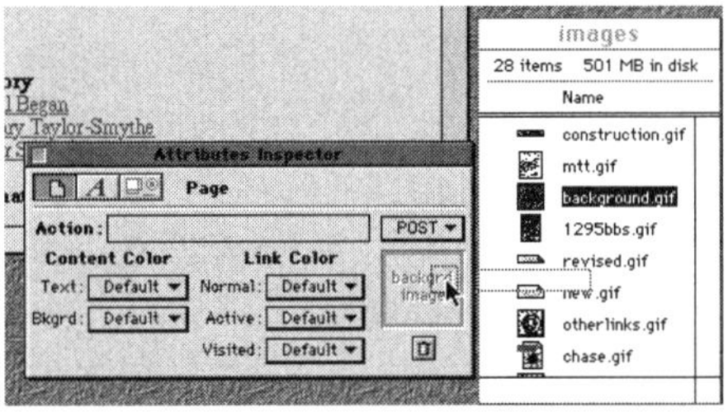

Figure 9. *Drag the Finder icon for an image onto the Backgrd Image area.*

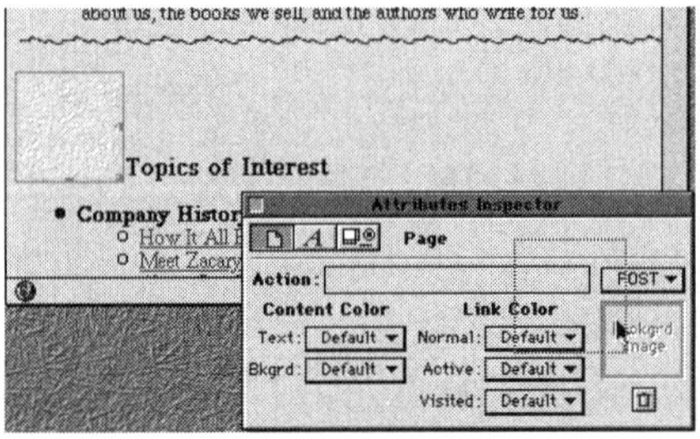

Figure 10. *Or drag an image from the Page window onto the Backgrd Image area.*

To add a background image with the Image view window

1. If the image is in a PageMill window, double-click it.

   or

   If the image is on disk, choose Open from the File menu and use the Open dialog box that appears to open it.

   The image opens in Image view.
2. Drag the Image icon from the Image view window to the Page icon in the Page window (see **Figure 12**).

When you release the mouse button, the image becomes a repeating pattern in the background of the page.

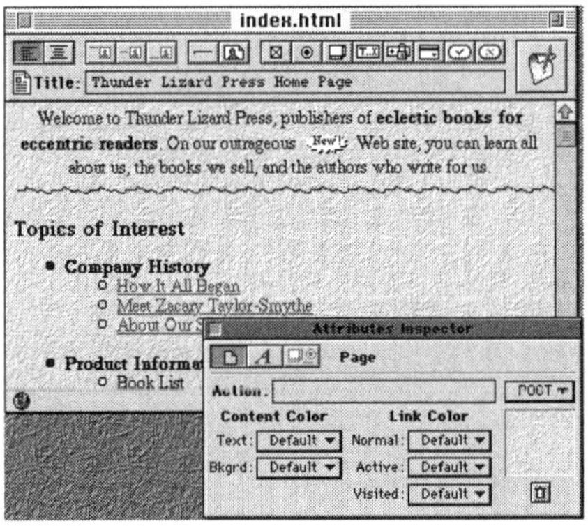

Figure 11. *The image becomes a background pattern.*

Figure 12. *You can also drag the Image icon onto the Page icon.*

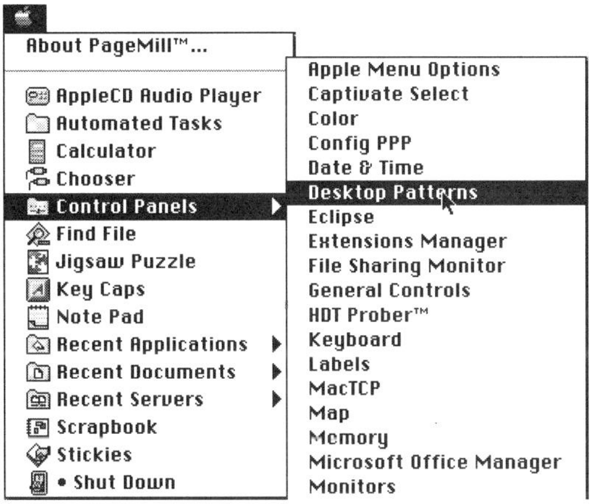

Figure 13. *Choose Desktop Patterns from the Control Panels submenu.*

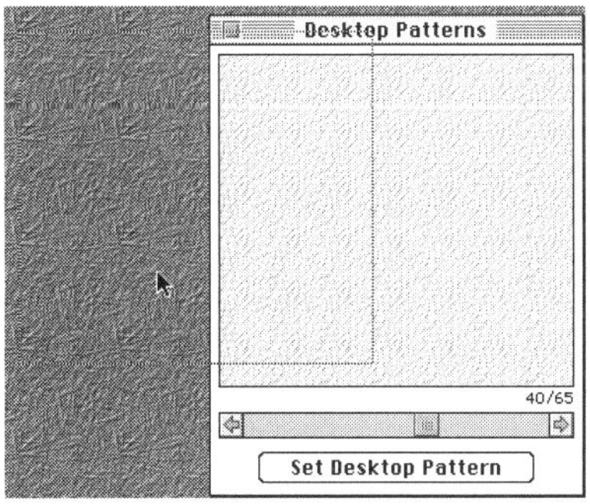

Figure 14. *Drag the pattern onto the Desktop…*

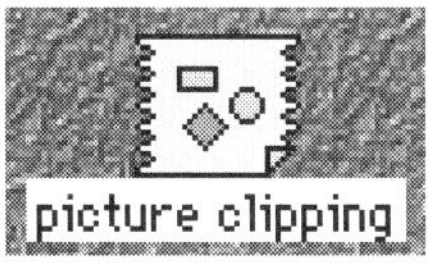

Figure 15. *…to create a picture clipping file.*

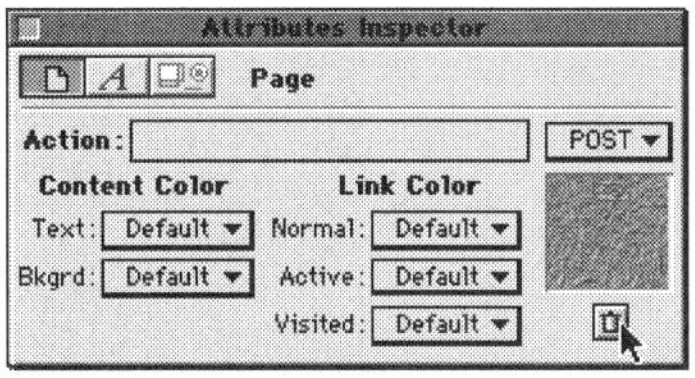

Figure 16. *Click the trash can icon in the Attributes Inspector to remove a background image.*

To use a desktop pattern as a background image

1. Choose Desktop Patterns from the Control Panels submenu under the Apple menu (see **Figure 13**).
2. In the Desktop Patterns window that appears, use the scroll bar to display the pattern you want to use as a background image.
3. Drag the image you want out of the Desktop Patterns window and onto the desktop (see **Figure 14**) or into a Finder folder icon or window.

   A picture clipping icon appears (see **Figure 15**). This is a file containing a PICT version of the desktop pattern.
4. Follow the steps on the previous page under “To add a background image with the Attributes Inspector” to drag the picture clipping icon onto the Backgrd Image area in the Attributes Inspector.

✔ Tips

- To follow the above steps, you must have System 7.5 or later properly installed on your Macintosh.
- Desktop patterns make excellent background patterns for Web pages since they’re small and most of them are textures that make seamless patterns. Use them as they are or open them in a graphics application like Photoshop to change brightness and contrast.

To remove a background image

Click the tiny trash can icon beneath the Backgrd Image area in the Attributes Inspector (see **Figure 16**).

The image and background disappear.

About Background Colors

The default background color for a Web page is light gray. You can change this, however, to be almost any color you like.

✔ Tips

- Although background colors are normally used instead of background images, they can be used effectively together if the background image has a transparent background. I tell you how to make image backgrounds transparent in **Chapter 5**.
- If the background color you select is similar to the text or link colors, text will be difficult to read. I tell you about changing text color on the following pages.

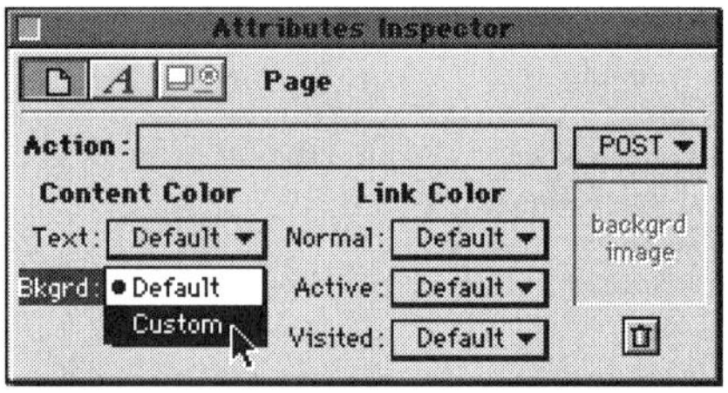

Figure 17. *Choose Custom from the Bkgrd pop-up menu…*

To specify a background color

1. Choose Show Attributes Inspector from the Window menu or press ⌘;.
2. Click the Page button to display the Attributes Inspector's Page options (see **Figure 8**).
3. Choose Custom from the Bkgrd pop-up menu (see **Figure 17**).
4. Use the standard color wheel that appears (see **Figure 18**) to choose a color for the background. Then click OK or press Return or Enter in the color wheel window to dismiss it.

The color you selected appears on the Bkgrd pop-up menu (see **Figure 19**) and becomes the background color.

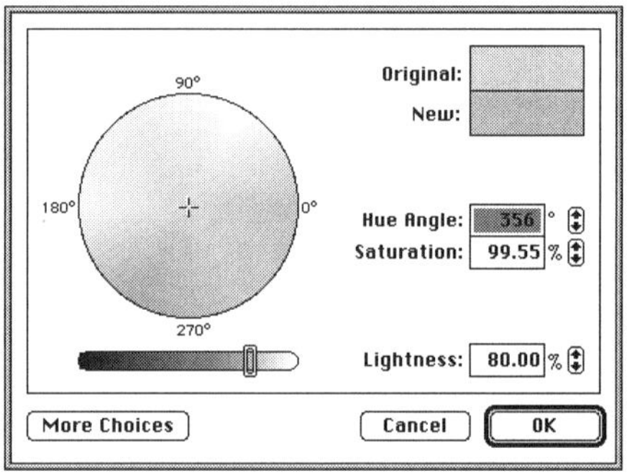

Figure 18. *…to display a standard color wheel.*

Figure 19. *The color you selected appears on the menu.*

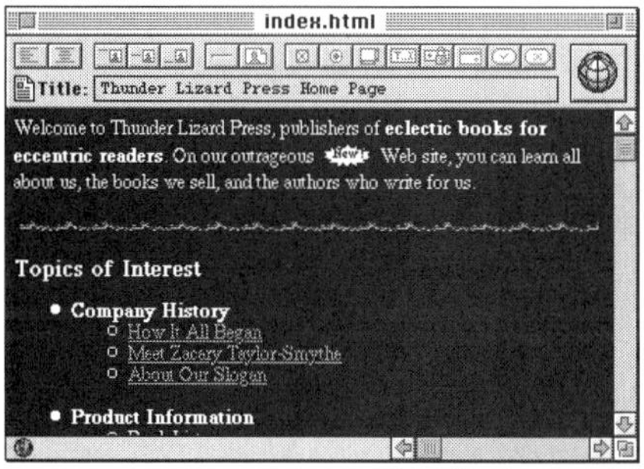

Figure 20. *For an interesting effect, try light text on a dark background.*

To restore the default background color

1. Follow the instructions above to display the Page options of the Attributes Inspector.
2. Choose Default from the Bkgrd pop-up menu.

The background returns to the default gray color.

About Text & Link Colors

PageMill lets you specify custom colors for all text that appears on the page:

- Text Content is the text that is not a link. The default color is black.
- Normal link is a link to a page that has not yet been viewed. The default color is blue.
- Active link is a link as it is being clicked. The default color is red.
- Visited Link is a link to a page that has already been viewed. The default color is purple.

✔ Tips

- If text or link color is too similar to background color or background image color, text will be difficult to read. I tell you how to change background images and colors on the previous pages.
- Text color can usually be overridden with Preferences options within a Web browser. This means the colors you specify may not be the ones that appear for everyone who views the page.
- For an interesting effect, try white or light colored text on a black or dark colored background (see **Figure 20**).

To specify text & link colors

1. Choose Show Attributes Inspector from the Window menu or press ⌘;.
2. Click the Page button to display the Attributes Inspector's Page options (see **Figure 8**).
3. Choose Custom from the pop-up menu for the type of text you want to change (see **Figure 21**).
4. Use the standard color wheel that appears (see **Figure 18**) to choose a color for the background. Then click OK or press Return or Enter in the color wheel window to dismiss it.

   The color you selected appears on the pop-up menu (see **Figure 22**) and becomes the text or link color.
5. Repeat steps 3 and 4 for each text or link color you want to change.

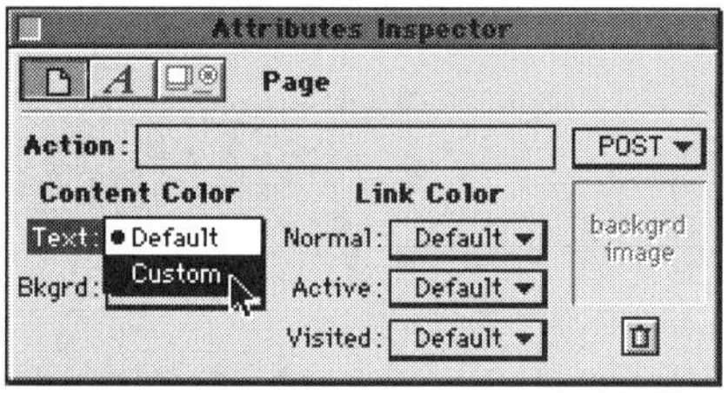

Figure 21. *Choose Custom from a text or link pop-up menu.*

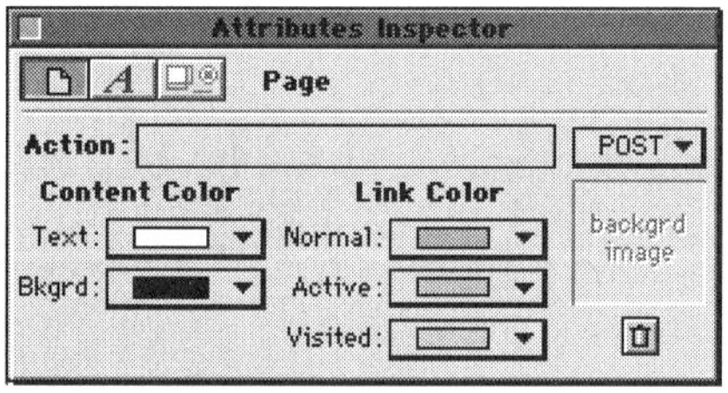

Figure 22. *The colors you chose appear on the pop-up menus.*

To restore the default text or link color

1. Follow the instructions above to display the Page options of the Attributes Inspector.
2. Choose Default from the pop-up menu for the type of text you want to change.

   The text you changed returns to the default color.
3. Repeat step 2 for each text or link color you want to restore to the default color.

9 TESTING & ENHANCING PAGES

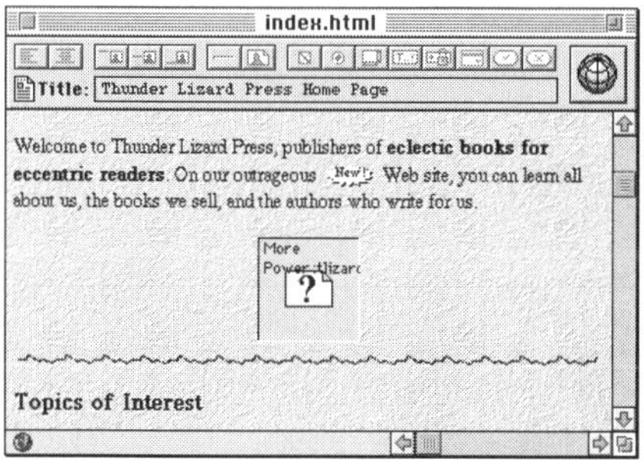

Figure 1. *Use PageMill's Preview view to find missing images…*

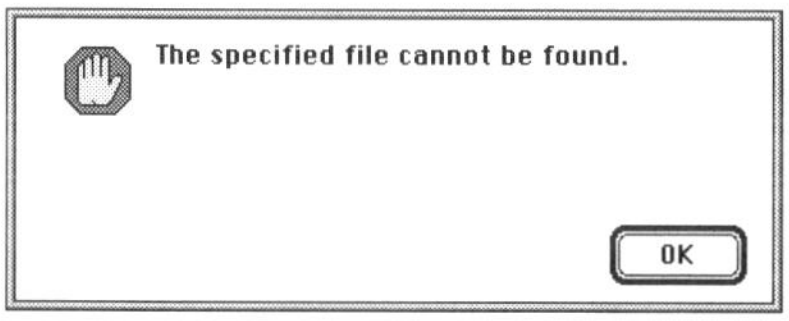

Figure 2. *…or incorrect URLs.*

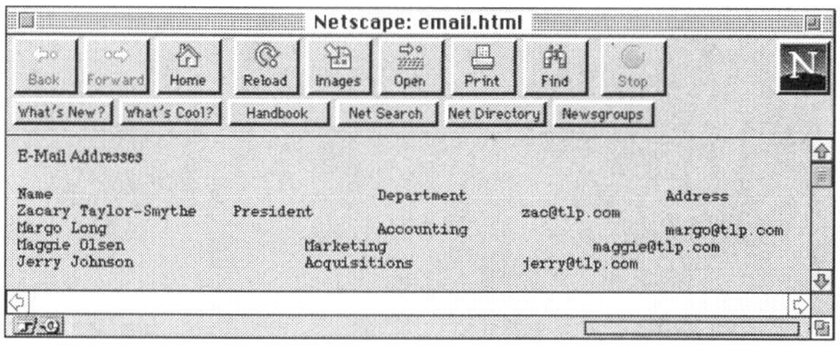

Figure 3. *Open pages with a variety of Web browsers to avoid formatting surprises.*

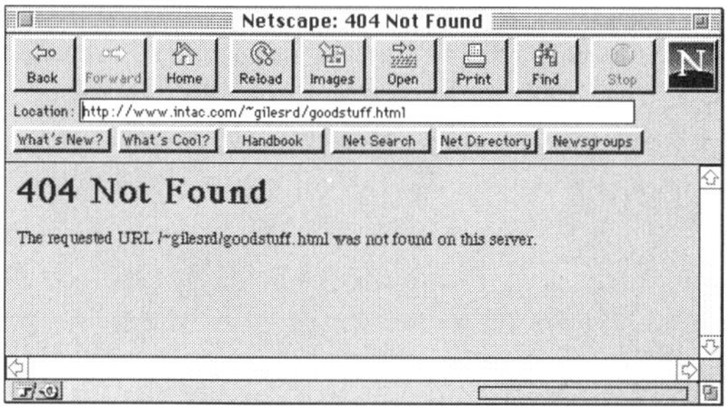

Figure 4. *Use a Web browser and Internet connection to test external links.*

About Testing Pages

Even after you've put the finishing touches on your Web pages, they may not be ready for installation on your Web server. There's one last thing you need to do: test them.

The testing process should include the following procedures:

- Use PageMill's Preview view to view pages and test all local links. This is how you can learn about missing images (see **Figure 1**) or incorrect URLs on your site (see **Figure 2**).
- Open the pages with a variety of Web browsers to make sure they look the way you expect them to. This is how you can avoid formatting surprises (see **Figure 3**).
- Use your favorite Web browser to test external links. This is how you can learn about incorrect URLs for pages that aren't on your site (see **Figure 4**).

✔ Tip

- In reality, the testing process never ends. Even if you never change a thing on your Web site, other sites change regularly. If your pages include external links, it's important that you test them regularly. That's the only way you can be sure that the linked pages are still available on an ever-changing Internet.

To view pages in Preview view

1. Choose Save from the File menu or press ⌘S to save changes to the page you want to test.
2. Choose Close from the File menu or press ⌘W to close the file you want to test.
3. Choose Open from the file menu or press ⌘O. Use the standard Open dialog box that appears to locate and open the file you want to test.
4. Check the Toggle Preview Mode button (see **Figure 5**) to make sure you are looking at the page in Preview view (see **Figure 6**). If not, click the button to switch to Preview view.

Figure 5. *Use the Toggle Preview Mode button to switch from Page view to Preview view and back.*

✔ Tips

- I tell you how to use the Save, Close, and Open commands in **Chapter 2**.
- Although it's possible to simply switch to Preview view without following the first three steps above, PageMill will sometimes display a page differently when you when you close it and then reopen it. Reopening a page is the only surefire way to get a true preview of it.
- Although PageMill's Preview view closely simulates a Web browser, it is not a true Web browser. The only way to see what a page would look like when viewed with a specific browser is to open and view it with that browser. I tell you how later in this chapter.

Figure 6. *Preview view gives you a good idea of what your page will look like on the Web—and gives you an opportunity to test all local links.*

To test pages in Preview view

1. Follow the instructions on the previous page to open the page you want to test.
2. Scroll through the page to make sure the images appear the way you want them to.
3. One by one, click each of the links on the page to ensure that they open the appropriate pages.
4. Click each "hot spot" of each image map to make sure all hot spots display the appropriate pages.

Figure 7. *The mouse pointer turns into a pointing hand when positioned over a link.*

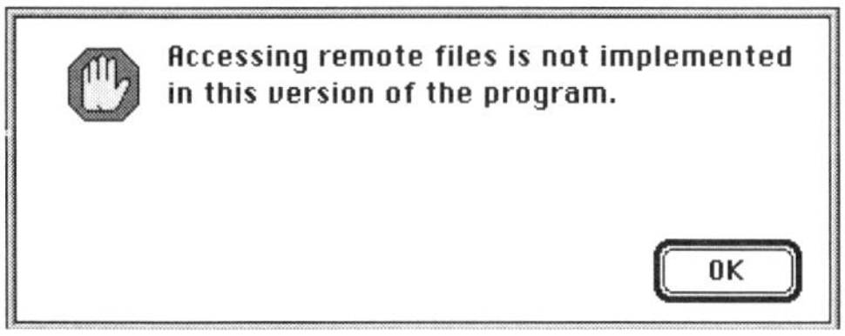

Figure 8. *If you click an external link, PageMill reminds you that it can't access remote files.*

✔ Tips

- If an image is missing from a page, an Image Not Found icon appears in its place (see **Figure 1**).
- When you position the mouse pointer over a link in Preview view, the mouse pointer turns into hand with a pointing finger. The address or URL for the link appears in the Link Location Bar at the bottom of the window. You can see all this in **Figure 7**.
- If you click a link to an external document, PageMill displays a dialog box like the one in **Figure 8**. These are links you'll have to check with your Web browser. I tell you how later in this chapter.
- As you uncover problems with your pages, you can switch to Page or Edit view to fix them. Click on the Toggle Preview Mode button to switch back and forth. The information throughout this book should help you solve any problems you might encounter.
- When you're finished fixing problems you found while testing a page, start the testing process from scratch to make sure you really fixed them all—and didn't create new ones.

To open pages with a Web browser

In the Finder, drag the icon for the page you want to view on top of the application icon for the Web browser with which you want to view it (see **Figure 9**). If the program isn't already running, it will launch.

or

Launch the Web browser application with which you want to view the page and use the Open or Open File command under its File menu to locate and open the page you want to view.

A window containing the Web page will appear.

Figures 10, **11**, and **12** show the page from **Figure 6** when viewed with three different Web browsers. Note the subtle differences.

✔ Tips

- You do not need an Internet connection to open and view a Web page file on your hard disk with a Web browser.
- Test your pages with as many Web browsers as you can to get a good idea of all the appearance possibilities.

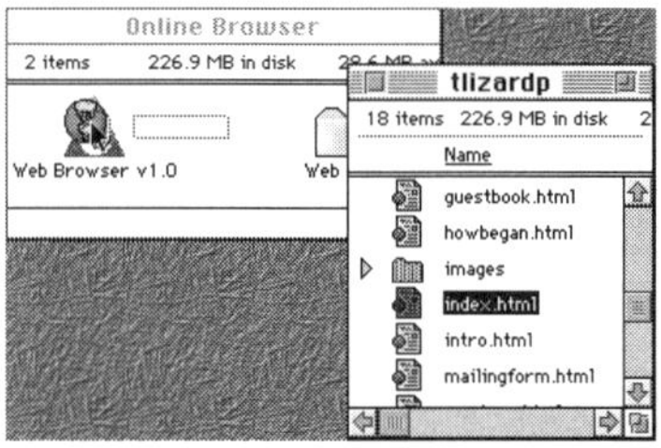

Figure 9. *Drag the page file's icon onto the browser's icon.*

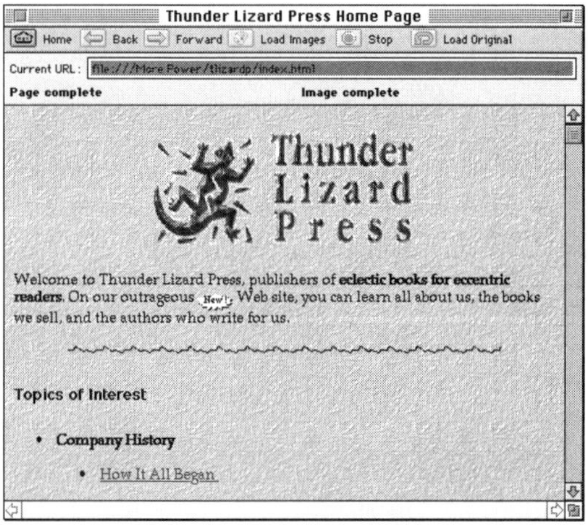

Figure 10. *Here's what a page looks like when opened with America Online's browser,…*

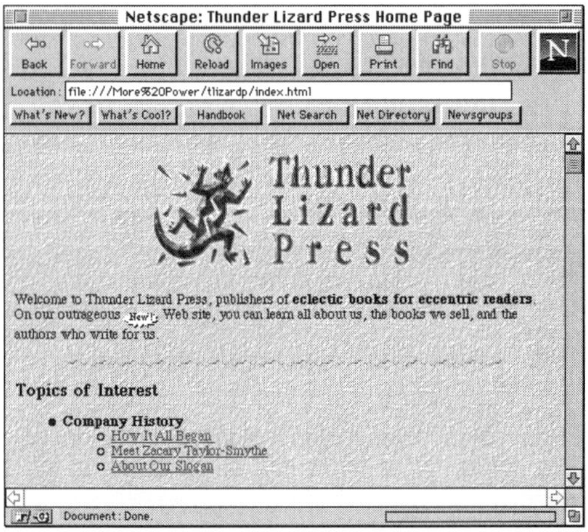

Figure 11. *…Netscape Navigator,…*

Figure 12. *…and MacWeb.*

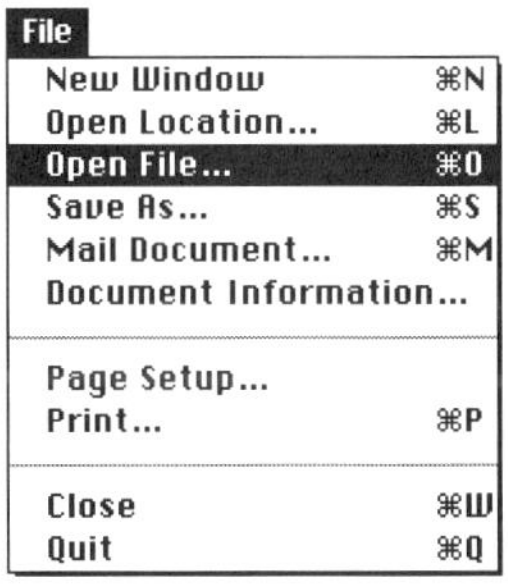

Figure 13. *A Web browser's file menu should offer a command to open a Web page file on disk.*

To test external links

1. Launch your Web browser and establish a connection to the Internet.
2. Choose Open or Open File from the browser's File menu (see **Figure 13**).
3. Use the Standard Open dialog box that appears to locate and open the page containing the external links you want to test.
4. One by one, click each of the external links on the page to ensure that they open the appropriate pages on the World Wide Web. Use the browser's Back command or button to quickly return to the page you're testing.
5. Click each image map "hot spot" with an external link to make sure they display the appropriate pages on the World Wide Web.

✔ Tips

- You must have an Internet connection to check external links.
- You must use a regular Web browser to check external links. If you try to test an external link with PageMill's Preview mode, a dialog box like the one in **Figure 8** will appear.
- Each external link that is successfully tested will turn purple or the custom color you may have specified for visited links.
- The File menu in **Figure 13** is for Netscape Navigator. If you use a different browser, the menu or command name may differ.
- As you uncover problems with your pages, you can switch to PageMill and use its Page or Edit view to fix and save them. I tell you about links in **Chapter 6**. Then use the browser's Reload command or button to reload the page from disk and test again.

About Page Enhancements

Although PageMill supports the writing and previewing of HTML version 2.0 markup tags and some Netscape extensions to HTML version 2.0, there are a variety of new, powerful tags that PageMill does not yet support. That doesn't mean, however, that you can't use these tags and extensions. On the contrary—PageMill's Raw HTML "style" lets you enter any tags you like. This makes it possible to enhance your pages to include formatting and features that cannot be automatically included by PageMill.

Figure 14 shows an example of a Web page that includes a table made with HTML 3.0 tags that are not supported by PageMill. **Figure 15** shows how that page appears in PageMill's Page view.

✔ Tips

- **Appendix D** at the end of this book provides a list of the HTML tags and extensions that PageMill supports, as well as some newer tags and extensions that might interest advanced PageMill users.
- You can use PageMill to open pages created by any HTML editor or Web publishing tool. If PageMill encounters tags it does not recognize, it automatically formats them as Raw HTML and displays them in red (see **Figure 15**).
- Although PageMill doesn't support every HTML tag, most browsers don't support them all either. If you use PageMill to create your Web pages and don't enhance them with unsupported tags and extensions, you're more likely to produce pages that will appear relatively the same with all browsers.
- "Enhanced for Netscape" is a phrase that refers to a Web page that includes Netscape extensions.

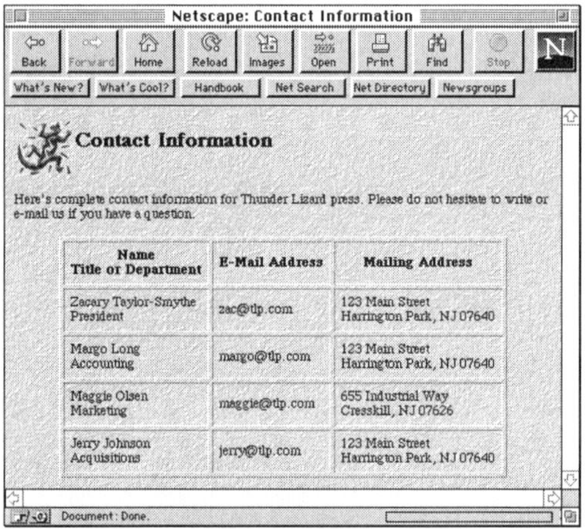

Figure 14. *Although Netscape Navigator properly displays Web pages using table-related commands…*

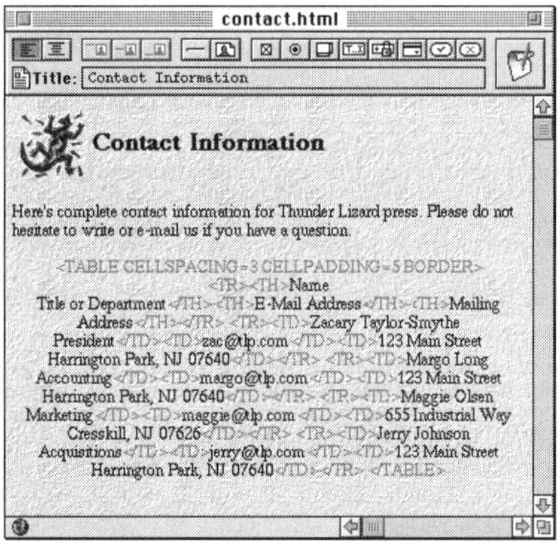

Figure 15. *…here's how PageMill displays them.*

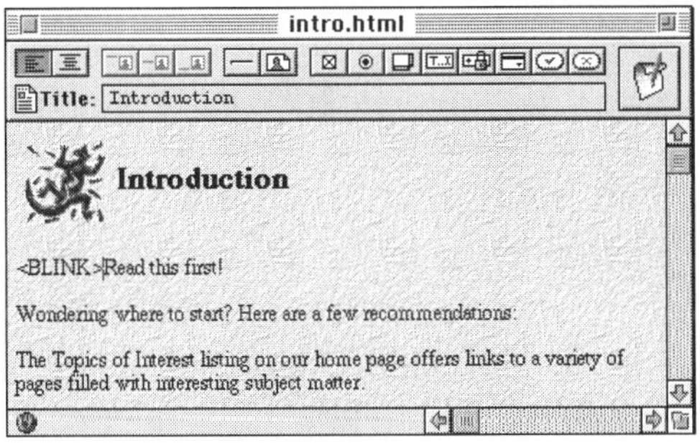

Figure 16. *Enter HTML tags where you want them to appear.*

Figure 17. *Select the tag.*

Figure 18. *When you choose Raw HTML from the Style menu, the tag turns red.*

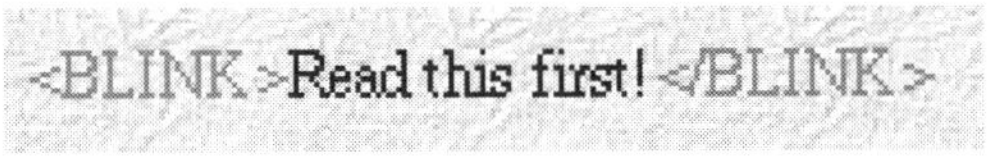

Figure 19. *Here's an example of the BLINK tag, which is not supported by PageMil, entered into a PageMill document.*

To enter Raw HTML into PageMill pages

1. Enter the HTML tags where you want them to appear, using standard text entry and editing techniques (see **Figure 16**). I tell you how to enter and edit text in **Chapter 2**.
2. Select the HTML tags (see **Figure 17**).
3. Choose Raw HTML from the Style menu.

   or

   Press Shift ⌘ H.

   The selected text turns red (see **Figure 18**).
4. Repeat steps 1 through 3 for all the HTML tags you want to enter directly into PageMill.

Figure 19 shows an example of the <BLINK>...</BLINK> tags, which are not supported by PageMill.

✔ Tip

■ If desired, you can apply Raw HTML style to a block of text that combines unrecognized HTML tags with recognized tags and plain text. Save the page, close it, and reopen it. PageMill automatically sorts out the tags and text and applies the Raw HTML style to only those tags it does not recognize.

To test Raw HTML tags

1. Choose Save from the File menu or press [⌘S] to save all changes to the page file you want to view.
2. In the Finder, drag the icon for the page you want to view on top of the application icon for a Web browser that supports the HTML tags you used. If the program isn't already running, it will launch.

   or

   Launch the Web browser application with which you want to view the page and use the Open or Open File command under its File menu to locate and open the page you want to view.

A window containing the web page will appear.

Figures 20 and **21** show the page from **Figure 19** when opened with two different browsers.

✔ Tips

- Although PageMill always displays unrecognized tags as Raw HTML, any browser that understands the tags will interpret them correctly (see **Figure 20**).
- Most browsers will ignore tags they cannot recognize (see **Figure 21**).
- As shown in **Figure 22**, if a browser ignores certain tags that you've used on a page, the results can be catastrophic.

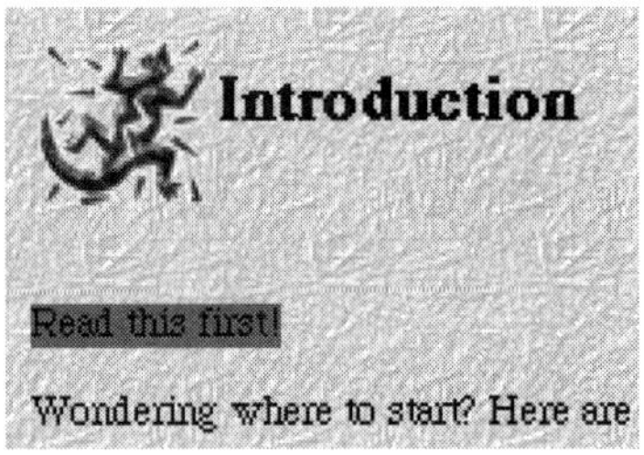

Figure 20. *Netscape Navigator, which recognizes the BLINK tag, properly displays the blinking text…*

Figure 21. *…while America Online's browser, which does not recognize the BLINK tag text, ignores it.*

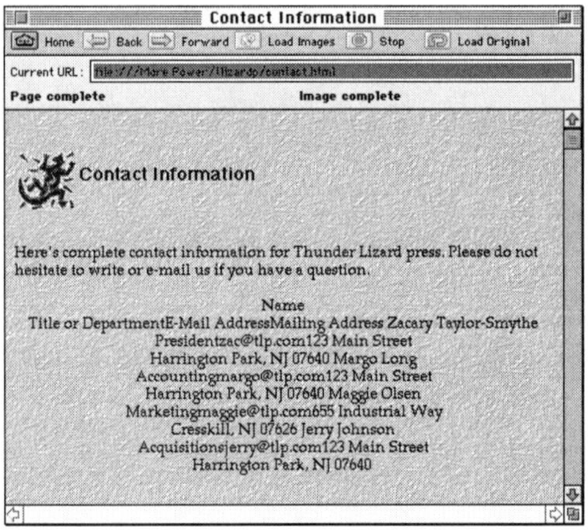

Figure 22. *Here's the page from Figures 14 and 15 when viewed with America Online's Browser. As this illustrates, ignoring tags can lead to very undesirable results.*

To edit PageMill page files with a text editor

1. In the Finder, drag the icon for the page file you want to edit on top of the application icon for a text editor or word processor. If the program isn't already running, it will launch.

   or

   Launch the text editor or word processor application with which you want to edit the page and use the Open command under its File menu to locate and open the page you want to edit.

   The page opens in a document window (see **Figure 23**).
2. Make desired changes to HTML tags and text.
3. Choose Save from the File menu to save your changes.

intro.html

```
<HTML>
<HEAD>
   <TITLE>Introduction</TITLE>
</HEAD>
<BODY BACKGROUND="images/background.gif">
<H2><IMG SRC="images/image6.gif" WIDTH="52" HEIGHT="52"
NATURALSIZEFLAG=
"0" ALIGN=middle>Introduction</H2>
<BR>
<BLINK>Read this first!</BLINK><BR>
<BR>
Wondering where to start? Here are a few recommendations:<BR>
<BR>
The Topics of Interest listing on our home page offers links to a
variety
of pages filled with interesting subject matter.
</BODY>
</HTML>
```

Figure 23. *Here's the page from* Figure 16 *when viewed with SimpleText.*

✔ Tips

- You need a good, solid knowledge of HTML to make major changes to PageMill-generated HTML documents.
- By viewing and experimenting with the underlying HTML code for pages you create with PageMill, you can learn more about HTML.

About Web Page Installation

Once your pages have been created, tested, and perhaps enhanced, they're ready to be installed on your Web server.

- If your Web server is accessible through an internal network, and you can mount its hard disk on your Macintosh desktop, you can install the page and image files you created by simply dragging them into the proper folders.
- If your Web server is accessible only by File Transfer Protocol (FTP), you'll need to use a program like Fetch to copy the page and image files from your hard disk into the proper folders on the server's hard disk.

Your Webmaster or System Administrator can provide more information about copying your Web pages and image files to the server.

✔ Tips

- If you do not install your completed pages on a Web server, they will not be accessible to anyone but you.
- If your Web server is not connected to the Internet through an Internet Service Provider (ISP), your pages will not be accessible to the World Wide Web.
- The instructions on the following pages are far from thorough. There are too many possible configurations to discuss them all in this book. Ask your Webmaster or System Administrator for specific instructions if you need more help.

To copy files over a network to a Web server

1. Use the Chooser to mount the Web server's hard disk. Its icon should appear on your desktop (see **Figure 24**).
2. Open the remote root directory on the server's hard disk. (This is the folder in which your page files will reside.)
3. Open the folder on your hard disk where your pages have been saved.
4. Select the files for the pages you want to copy and drag their icons to the window for the remote root directory (see **Figure 25**).

   A copy dialog box appears, indicating copy progress. Wait until it disappears before you continue.
5. Open the images folder in the remote root directory window. (This is the folder in which your image files will reside.)
6. Select the files for the images you want to copy and drag their icons to the window for the images folder inside the remote root directory.

   A copy dialog box appears, indicating copy progress. Wait until it disappears before you continue.
7. When you're finished, drag the server's hard disk icon to the trash to unmount it and close all its windows.

Figure 24. *When you mount the server's hard disk, its icon appears on your desktop.*

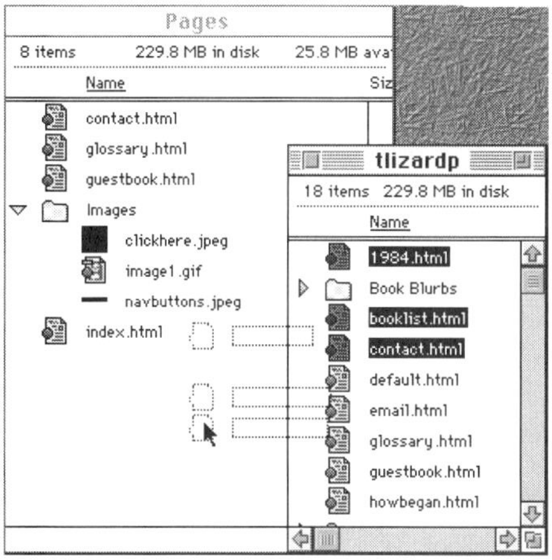

Figure 25. *Drag the file icons to the remote root directory window of the server hard disk to copy them.*

✔ Tip

- It's vital that the relationship between page files, image files, and folders is the same on the server as it is on your hard disk. For example, if images files are inside a folder called Images in the folder containing your Web pages on your hard disk, they must also be inside a folder called Images in the folder containing your Web pages on the server.

To copy files to a Web server with Fetch

1. Launch Fetch and establish a connection to the Internet.
2. Use the Open Connection dialog box (see **Figure 26**) to enter the Host Name, User ID, Password, and Directory for the remote root directory.
3. Choose Put Files and Folders from the Remote menu.
4. In the Put Files dialog box that appears, locate and add all the page files you want to copy to the remote root directory (see **Figure 27**). Then click Done.
5. If a Choose Formats dialog box appears (see **Figure 28**), choose Raw Data from both pop-up menus. Then click OK.
6. Wait while your files are uploaded to the server.
7. In the main Fetch window (see **Figure 29**), locate and open the folder in which your images will be stored.
8. Choose Put Files and Folders from the Remote menu.
9. In the Put Files dialog box that appears, locate and add all the image files you want to copy to the remote root directory. Then click Done.
10. If a Choose Formats dialog box appears, choose Raw Data from both pop-up menus. Then click OK.
11. Wait while your files are uploaded to the server.
12. When you're finished, choose Quit from Fetch's File menu to quit.

✔ Tip

- For more information about Fetch or to obtain a copy, check *http://www.dartmouth.edu/pages/softdev/fetch.html.*

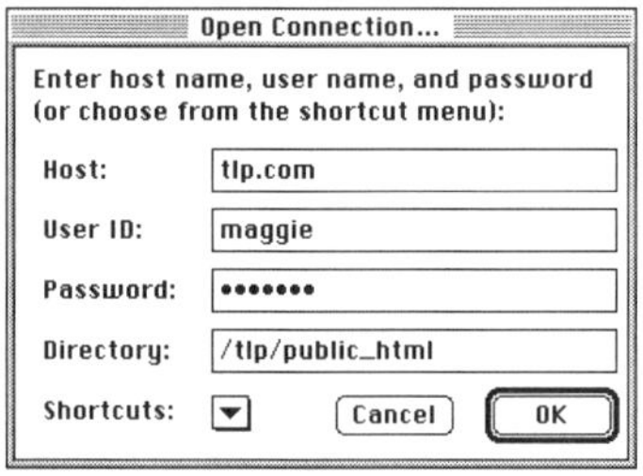

Figure 26. *Use the Open connection dialog box to connect to the Web server.*

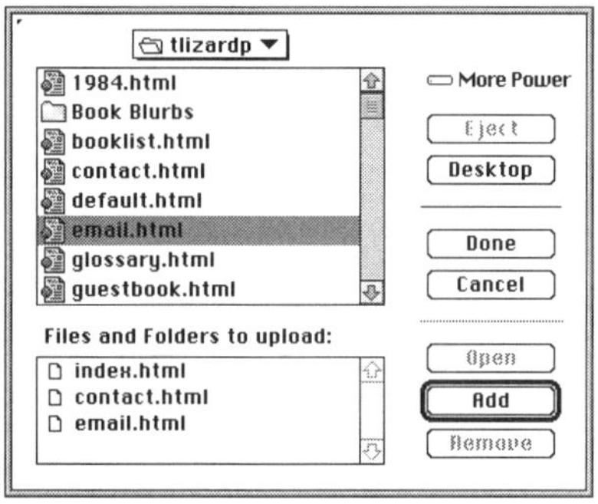

Figure 27. *Use the Put Files dialog box to select the files you want to copy to the server.*

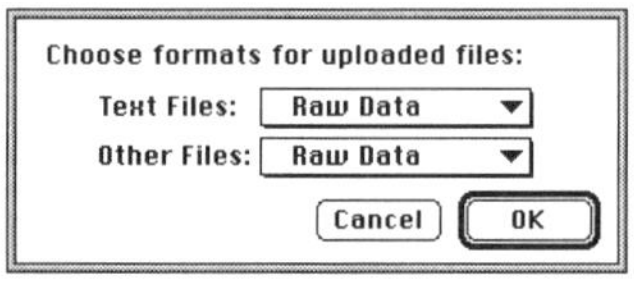

Figure 28. *Choose Raw Data as a format for files.*

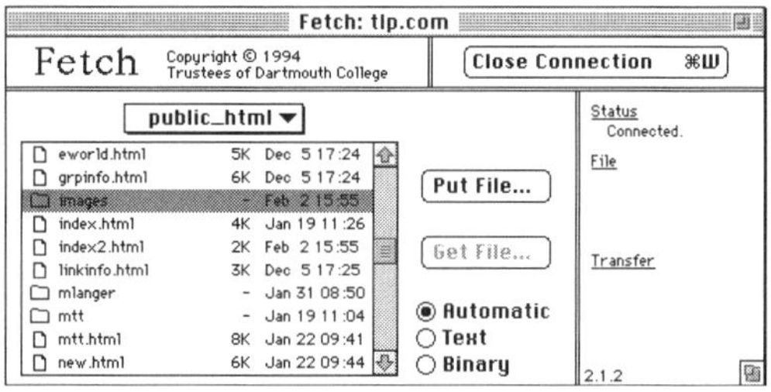

Figure 29. *Use the main Fetch window to open folders within the remote root directory.*

MENUS & COMMAND KEY EQUIVALENTS

A

About Menus & Command Key Equivalents

This appendix illustrates all of PageMill's menus and provides a list of all Command key equivalents you can use with PageMill.

To use a Command key equivalent, hold down the modifier key(s) while pressing the letter, number, or punctuation key corresponding to the command. Using Command key equivalents is discussed in **Chapter 1**.

Modifier Keys

Menu Symbol	Keyboard Key	Key Name
⌘	⌘	Command
⇧	Shift	Shift
⌥	Option	Option
⌃	Control	Control

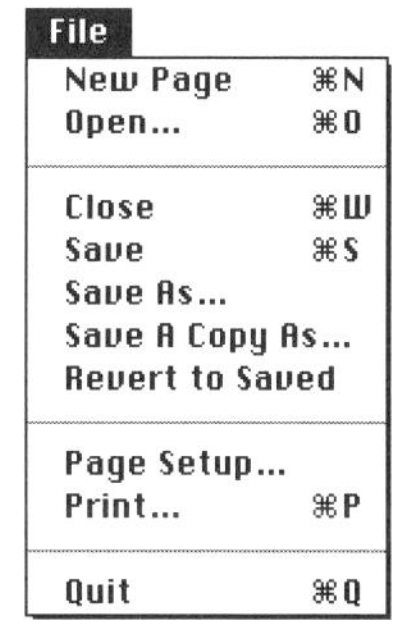

File Menu Commands

⌘ N	New Page
⌘ O	Open
⌘ W	Close
⌘ S	Save
⌘ P	Print
⌘ Q	Quit

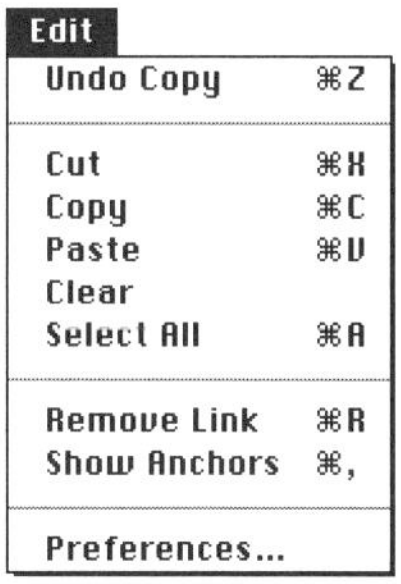

Edit Menu Commands

⌘ Z	Undo
⌘ X	Cut
⌘ C	Copy
⌘ V	Pastc
⌘ A	Select All
⌘ R	Remove Link
⌘ ,	Show Anchors

Style Menu Commands

Shift ⌘ P	Plain
⌘ B	Bold
⌘ I	Italic
Shift ⌘ T	Teletype
Shift ⌘ S	Strong
Shift ⌘ E	Emphasis
Shift ⌘ C	Citation
Shift ⌘ A	Sample
Shift ⌘ K	Keyboard
Shift ⌘ O	Code
Shift ⌘ V	Variable
Shift ⌘ H	Raw HTML

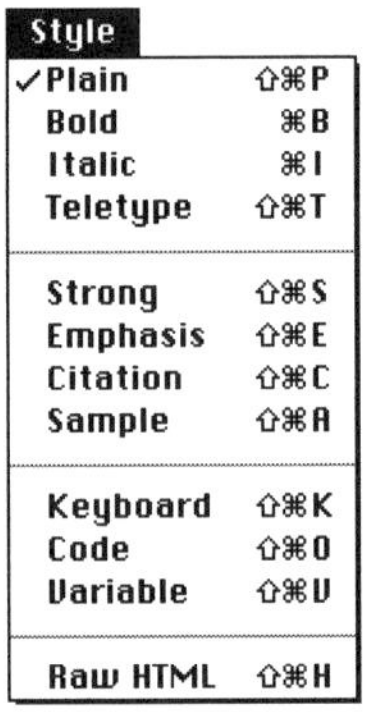

Format Menu Commands

⌘ [	Indent Left
⌘]	Indent Right
Option ⌘ P	Paragraph
Option ⌘ 6	Smallest Heading
Option ⌘ 5	Smaller Heading
Option ⌘ 4	Small Heading
Option ⌘ 3	Large Heading
Option ⌘ 2	Larger Heading
Option ⌘ 1	Largest Heading
Option ⌘ F	Preformatted
Option ⌘ B	Bullet List
Option ⌘ D	Directory List
Option ⌘ M	Menu List
Option ⌘ N	Numbered List
Option ⌘ E	Definition List
Option ⌘ T	Term List
Option ⌘ A	Address

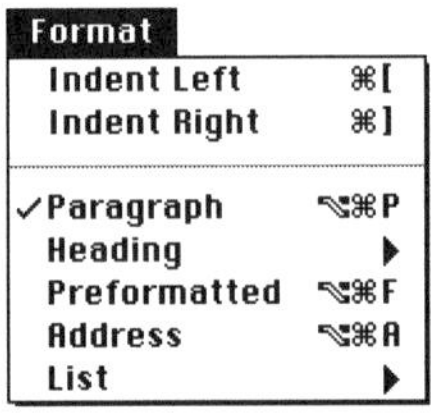

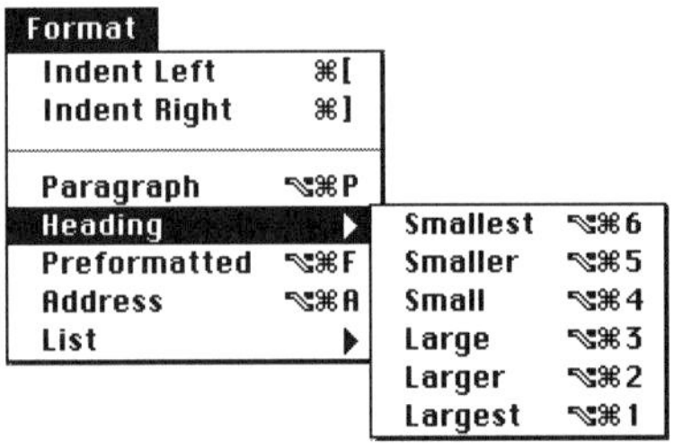

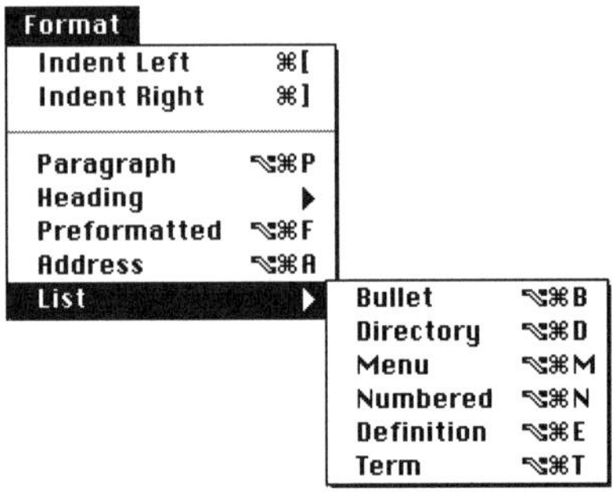

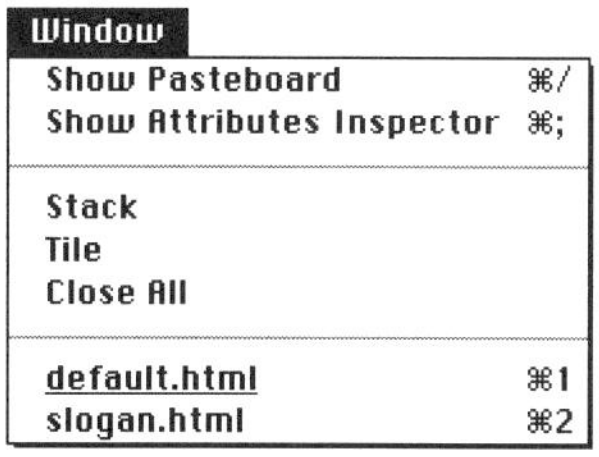

Window Menu Commands

⌘ /	Show Pasteboard
⌘ ;	Show Attributes Inspector
⌘ 1 - ⌘ 0	Show Corresponding Page Window (see menu)

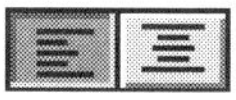

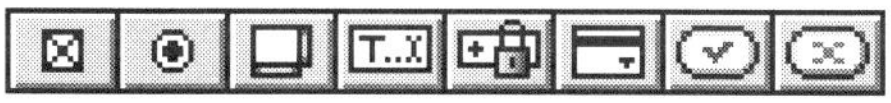

Button Commands

⌘ Control ←	Left Align Text
⌘ Control →	Right Align Text
⌘ Control ↑	Top Align Image
⌘ Control ↓	Bottom Align Image
⌘ Control ↑	Center Align Image (if image is top aligned)
⌘ Control ↓	Center Align Image (if image is bottom aligned)
⌘ Control 1	Insert Horizontal Rule
⌘ Control 2	Insert Image
⌘ Control 3	Insert Checkbox
⌘ Control 4	Insert Radio Button
⌘ Control 5	Insert Text Area
⌘ Control 6	Insert Text Field
⌘ Control 7	Insert Password Field
⌘ Control 8	Insert Popup
⌘ Control 9	Insert Submit Button
⌘ Control 0	Insert Reset Button
⌘ Control Spacebar	Toggle Preview Mode

BUTTONS, SWITCHES, & ICONS B

Page Button Bar Buttons

PageMill's button bar offers a variety of buttons for use with text, images, or forms in a page. For Command key equivalents for these buttons, see **Appendix A**.

Text alignment buttons

Left Align Text

Center Align Text

Image alignment buttons

Top Align Image

Center Align Image

Bottom Align Image

Insert graphic elements buttons

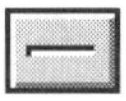
Insert Horizontal Rule

Insert Image

Insert form elements buttons

Insert Checkbox

Insert Radio Button

Insert Text Area

Insert Text Field

Insert Password Field

Insert Popup

Insert Submit Button

Insert Reset Button

Other PageMill Page Window Buttons & Icons

Toggle Preview Mode
(while in Page or Edit mode)

Toggle Preview Mode
(while in Preview mode)

Page Icon

URL Icon

Image View Buttons

A bar on the left side of the Image View window includes a number of buttons, switches, and icons for use when working with images.

Image Icon. The Image format (GIF or JPEG) appears beneath the icon.

Pointer Tool

Rectangle Hot Spot Tool

Circle Hot Spot Tool

Polygon Hot Spot Tool

Transparency Tool

Layering Tool. When clicked, the Layering pop-up menu appears.

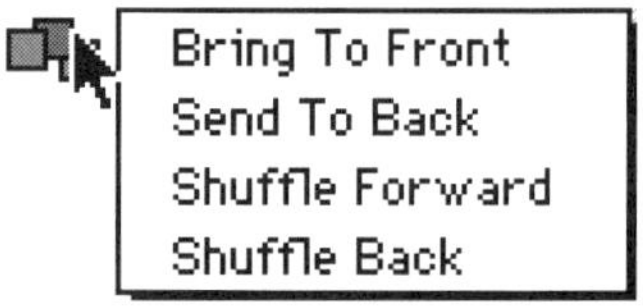

Hot Spot Color Icon. When clicked, the Hot Spot Color pop-up menu appears.

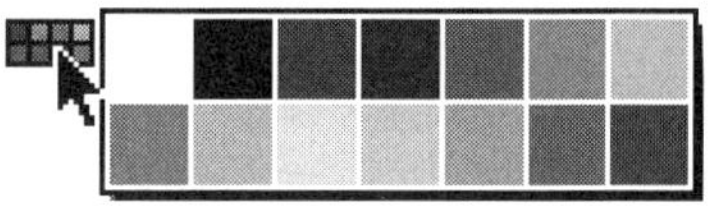

Hot Spot Label Switch (On)

Hot Spot Label Switch (Off)

Interlace Switch (On)

Interlace Switch (Off)

 Zoom In Button

 Zoom Out Button.

Attributes Inspector Button Bar Buttons

The Attributes Inspector has a small button bar that offers access to each category of attributes.

 Page Button

 Text Button

 Object Button

ATTRIBUTES INSPECTOR REFERENCE

C

About the Attributes Inspector

The Attributes Inspector provides a number of palettes filled with options to change Page, Text, and Object Attributes.

To display the Attributes Inspector, choose Show Attributes Inspector from the Window menu or press [⌘][;]. Click the Page, Text, or Object button to change the attributes of the active page or selected item. I tell you about using the Attributes Inspector throughout this book.

This appendix provides an illustrated guide to the Attributes Inspector's options. Although Page and Text options remain the same no matter what page is active or what text is selected, Object options vary depending on the kind of object selected.

Page Attributes

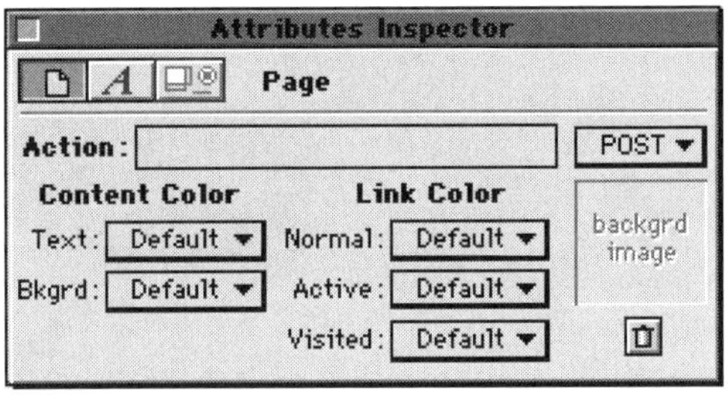

Page options, most of which are discussed in **Chapters 7** and **8**, let you change the appearance of a page and its text and associate a CGI with a form.

- **Action.** Use the edit box to enter the pathname for a CGI to launch on completion of a form on the page. Use the pop-up menu to select the method of exchanging information with the server: GET or POST. Enter information only if the page includes a form. If you are not sure what to enter, ask your Webmaster or System Administrator.
- **Content Color.** Use the Text and Bkgrd pop-up menus to choose Default or Custom. Default text color is black; default background color is gray. If you choose Custom, use the Color wheel that appears to choose the color you want.
- **Link Color.** Use the Normal, Active, and Visited pop-up menus to choose Default or Custom. Default Normal link color is blue; default Active link color is red; default Visited link color is purple. If you choose Custom, use the Color wheel that appears to choose the color you want.
- **Backgrd Image.** Drag an image into this area to use it as a background image or pattern.
- **Trash Icon.** Click this icon to remove a background image.

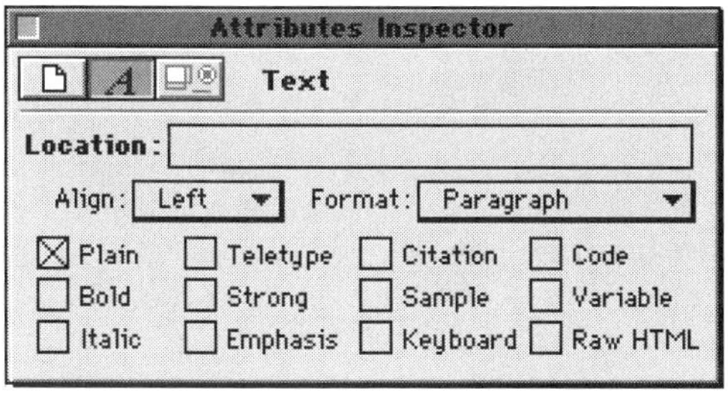

Text Attributes

Text options, most of which are discussed in **Chapters 3**, **4**, and **6**, let you change the appearance of selected text characters or paragraphs and create links.

- **Location.** Enter the address or URL for a page or other item to which you want to link the selected text.
- **Align.** Use this pop-up menu to choose Left or Center alignment for the selected paragraphs. The default value is Left.
- **Format.** Use this pop-up menu to select a format for the selected paragraphs. Options include Paragraph (the default), Preformatted, Smallest Heading, Smaller Heading, Small Heading, Large Heading, Larger Heading, Largest Heading, Bullet List, Directory List, Menu List, Numbered List, Definition List, and Term List.
- **Styles.** Use the check boxes in the bottom of the Attributes Inspector to turn character styles on or off for selected characters. Options include Plain (the default), Bold, Italic, Teletype, Strong, Emphasis, Citation, Sample, Keyboard, Code, Variable, and Raw HTML.

Image Attributes

Image options, most of which are discussed in **Chapter 5**, let you assign alternate text for an image and change its size, behavior, and border.

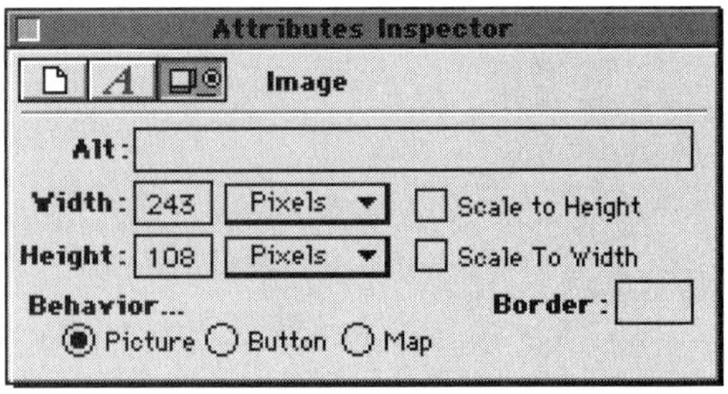

- **Alt.** Use this edit box to enter alternate text for the image. The text you enter will appear in text-based browsers or in graphic browsers that have the auto load image option turned off.
- **Width.** Use this edit box to specify an image width. Use the pop-up menu beside it to specify whether the measurement is in Pixels or a Percent of the original image size. This edit box and pop-up menu will only function if the Scale to Height check box is turned off.
- **Height.** Use this edit box to specify an image height. Use the pop-up menu beside it to specify whether the measurement is in Pixels or a Percent of the original image size. This edit box and pop-up menu will only function if the Scale to Width check box is turned off.
- **Scale to Height.** Turn on this check box to change the image width in proportion to its height.
- **Scale to Width.** Turn on this check box to change the image height in proportion to its width.
- **Border.** Enter a measurement, in pixels, to change the width of an image border. By default, this edit box is empty (no border) for images that behave as pictures.
- **Behavior.** Select one of the radio buttons—Picture, Button, or Map—to specify how the image is to be used on the page. The default selection is Picture.

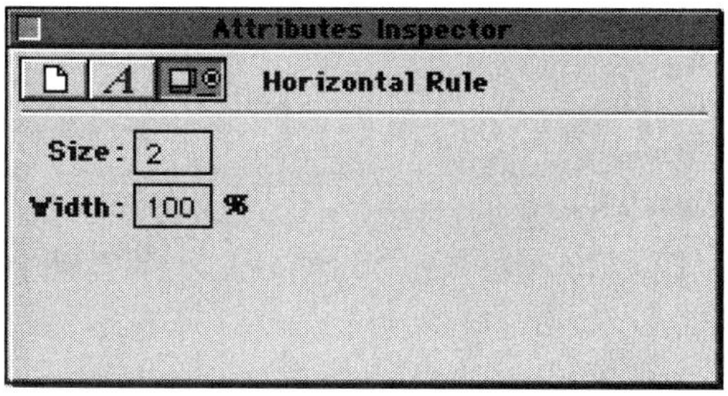

Horizontal Rule Attributes

Horizontal Rule options, most of which are discussed in **Chapter 5**, let you change the appearance of a selected horizontal rule.

- **Size.** Use this edit box to enter a thickness, in pixels, for the horizontal rule. The default value is 2.
- **Width.** Use this edit box to enter a horizontal width, as a percentage of the page width, for the horizontal rule. The default value is 100.

Checkbox Attributes

Checkbox options, which are discussed in **Chapter 7**, let you change the name, value, and default status of a check box. The name and value may be dependent on the CGI that will be used with the form, so check CGI documentation when changing these options.

- **Name.** Use this edit box to give the selected check box a name. The default value is checkbox.
- **Value.** Use this edit box to enter a value for the selected check box. The default value is check box.
- **Checked.** Use this check box to determine whether the selected check box is turned on by default. The default setting for this option is turned off.

Radio Button Attributes

Radio Button options, which are discussed in **Chapter 7**, let you change the name, value, and default status of a radio button. The name and value may be dependent on the CGI that will be used with the form, so check CGI documentation when changing these options.

- **Name.** Use this edit box to give the selected radio button a name. The default value is radio followed by a unique number for each group of radio buttons.
- **Value.** Use this edit box to enter a value for the selected radio button. The default value is radio.
- **Checked.** Use this check box to determine whether the selected radio button is selected by default. The default setting for this option is turned on for the last button in a group and turned off for all other buttons in the group. If you change this option for one radio button in a group, it will automatically change for one other button in the group since only one button in a group can be selected at a time.

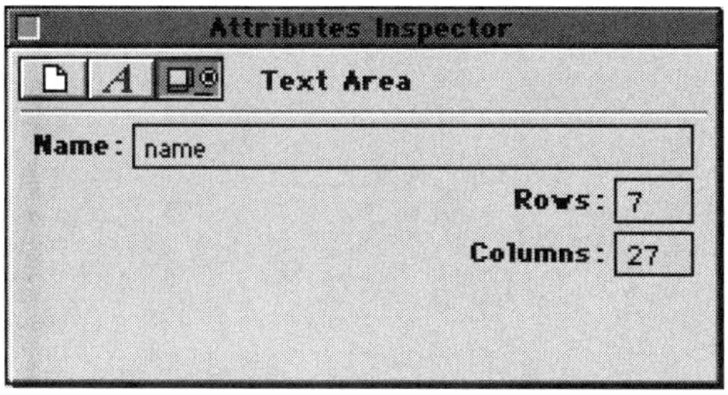

Text Area Attributes

Text Area options, which are discussed in **Chapter 7**, let you change the name and size of a text area. The name may be dependent on the CGI that will be used with the form, so check CGI documentation when changing this options.

- **Name.** Use this edit box to give the selected text area a name. The default value is name.
- **Rows.** Use this edit box to enter the number of text rows that should appear within the text area. The default value is 7.
- **Columns.** Use this edit box to enter the number of character columns that should appear within the text area. The default value is 27.

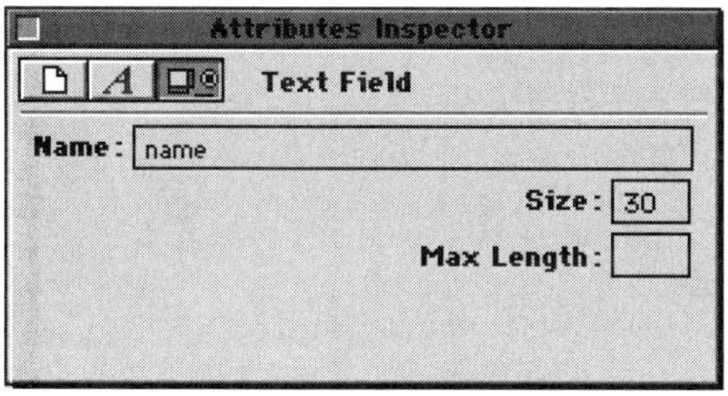

Text Field Attributes

Text Field options, which are discussed in **Chapter 7**, let you change the name, size, and maximum length of a text field. The name may be dependent on the CGI that will be used with the form, so check CGI documentation when changing this options.

- **Name.** Use this edit box to give the selected text field a name. The default value is name.
- **Size.** Use this edit box to enter the length, in characters, of the text field. The default value is 30.
- **Max Length.** Use this edit box to enter the maximum length, in characters, of an entry in the text field. By default, this edit box is empty.

Password Field Attributes

Password Field options, which are discussed in **Chapter 7**, let you change the name, size, and maximum length of a password field. The name may be dependent on the CGI that will be used with the form, so check CGI documentation when changing this options.

- **Name.** Use this edit box to give the selected password field a name. The default value is name.
- **Size.** Use this edit box to enter the length, in characters, of the password field. The default value is 30.
- **Max Length.** Use this edit box to enter the maximum length, in characters, of an entry in the password field. By default, this edit box is empty.

Selection Field Attributes

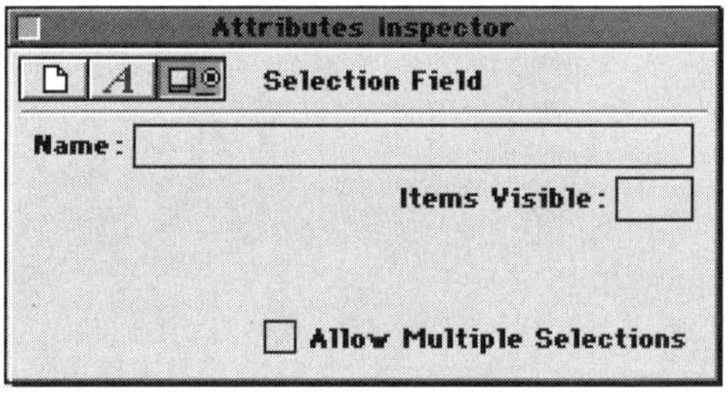

Selection Field options, which are discussed in **Chapter 7**, let you change the name, appearance, and functionality of pop-up menus and selection list fields. The name may be dependent on the CGI that will be used with the form, so check CGI documentation when changing this options.

- **Name.** Use this edit box to give the selected pop-up menu or selection list field a name. By default, this edit box is empty.
- **Items Visible.** Use this edit box to enter the number of items you want to appear in the selected scrolling list field. This determines the vertical size of the scrolling list. By default, this edit box is empty, which displays the object as a pop-up menu.
- **Allow Multiple Selections.** Use this check box to determine whether the selected scrolling list field should allow more than one selection. By default, this check box is turned off.

Submit Button Attributes

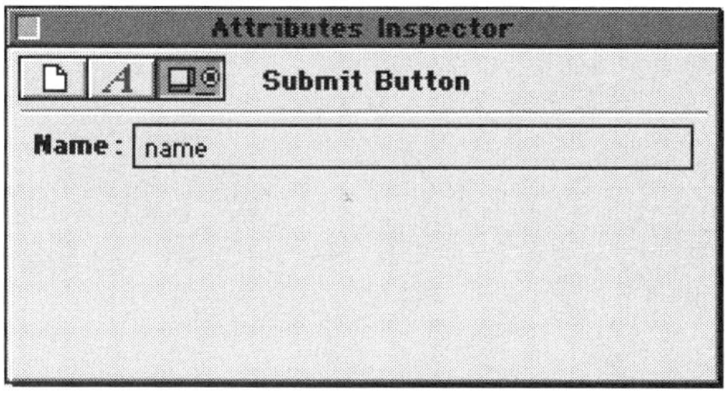

Submit Button options, which are discussed in **Chapter 7**, let you change the name of a submit button. The name may be dependent on the CGI that will be used with the form, so check CGI documentation when changing this options.

- **Name.** Use this edit box to give the selected submit button a name. The default value is name.

Reset Button Attributes

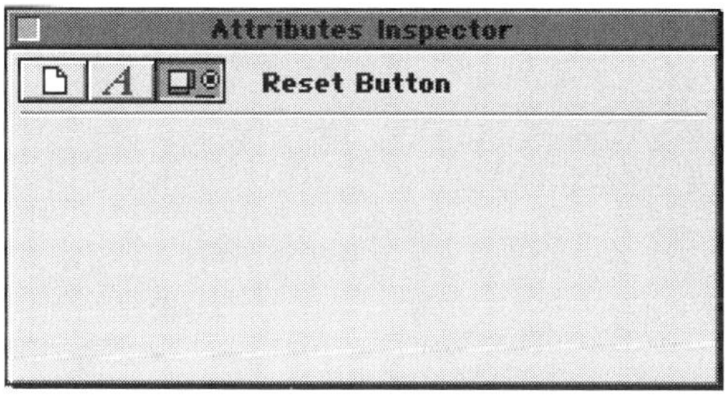

Although the Object options can be displayed for the Reset Button, which is discussed in **Chapter 7**, there are no options.

HTML REFERENCE D

About HTML

HyperText Markup Language (HTML) is a programming language that uses special codes called markup tags to indicate formatting and special elements within a Web page. Web browser software like Netscape Navigator, NCSA Mosaic, and the Web browsers that are part of eWorld and America Online interpret HTML tags to display HTML documents as Web pages with formatted text and graphics.

PageMill 1.0 supports version 2.0 of HTML, as well as several extensions to HTML that are recognized by Netscape and some other browsers.

This appendix provides a list of the HTML 2.0 markup tags and extensions that are supported by PageMill. It also includes many (but not all) additional tags and extensions that are not supported by PageMill.

This appendix is intended as a reference for PageMill users, not as an HTML tutorial. For step-by-step, fully illustrated instructions for using HTML, look for *HTML for the World Wide Web: Visual QuickStart Guide*, which is also published by Peachpit Press. For more information about HTML elements, use your Web browser to consult *http://www.sandia.gov/sci_compute/elements.html.*

Basic Page Tags

<DOCTYPE HTML PUBLIC "-//IETF//DTD HTML 2.0//EN">	Document prologue. [1]
<HTML>...</HTML>	Document type.
<TITLE>...</TITLE>	Page title.
<HEAD>...</HEAD>	Page header.
<BODY>...</BODY>	Page body.
<BODY BACKGROUND="url">...</BODY>	Page body with background URL specified.
<BODY BGCOLOR=#>...</BODY>	Page body with background color number specified.
<BODY TEXT=#>...</BODY>	Page body with text color number specified.
<BODY LINK=#>...</BODY>	Page body with link color number specified.
<BODY VLINK=#>...</BODY>	Page body with visited link color number specified.

<BODY ALINK=#>...</BODY> — Page body with active link color number specified.

<NEXTID N=#> — Identifier number used by automatic hypertext editors. [1]

<ISINDEX> — Identifies the page as searchable. [1]

<ISINDEX PROMPT="prompt"> — Specify prompt string for index search. [1]

<META CONTENT="text" — To embed document meta-information not defined by other HTML elements. [1]

<!--text--> — Comment. [1]

Paragraphs, Line Break, & Other Divider Tags

<P> — Paragraph. PageMill rewrites this as <BR>.

<P>...</P> — Paragraph. [3]

 — Line break.

<BR CLEAR=left|right|center> — Line break to the next area clear of floating graphics. [2]

<HR> — Horizontal rule.

<HR SIZE=#> — Horizontal rule with thickness specified in pixels.

<HR WIDTH=#%> — Horizontal rule with width specified as a percent.

<HR NOSHADE> — Horizontal rule with a solid line. [2]

<HR CLEAR=left|right|center> — Horizontal rule to the next area clear of floating graphics. [2]

<NOBR>...</NOBR> — Prevent word wrap. [2]

<WBR> — Allow word break in a NOBR area. [2]

Physical Style Tags

<PLAINTEXT>...</PLAINTEXT> — Plain style. [1]

<B>...</B> — Bold style.

<I>...</I> — Italic style.

<TT>...</TT> — Teletype style.

<S>...</S> — Strikeout style. [1]

<BLINK>...</BLINK> — Blinking text style. [2]

<FONT SIZE=#>...</FONT> — Specify Font Size. [2]

<FONT SIZE=+|-#>...</FONT> — Increase or Decrease Font Size. [2]

<BASEFONT SIZE=#> — Specify a base font size. [2]

<U>...</U> — Underline. [3]

Logical Style Tags

<STRONG>...</STRONG>	Strong emphasis.
<EM>...</EM>	Emphasis.
<CITE>...</CITE>	Citation.
<SAMP>...</SAMP>	Sample.
<KBD>...</KBD>	Keyboard.
<CODE>...</CODE>	Code.
<VAR>...</VAR>	Variable.
<DFN>...</DFN>	Definition. [1]

Text Alignment Tags

<CENTER>...</CENTER>	Center align text.
<P ALIGN=left|center|right>...</P>	Paragraph alignment. [3]
<H# ALIGN=left|center|right>...</H#>	Heading alignment. [3]

Paragraph Formats Tags

<H1>...</H1>	Heading 1
<H2>...</H2>	Heading 2
<H3>...</H3>	Heading 3
<H4>...</H4>	Heading 4
<H5>...</H5>	Heading 5
<H6>...</H6>	Heading 6
<PRE>...</PRE>	Preformatted
<PRE WIDTH=#>...</PRE>	Preformatted with width specified as a number. [1]
<XMP>...</XMP>	Preformatted. [1]
<LISTING>...</LISTING>	Preformatted (designed for lists). [1]
<ADDRESS>...</ADDRESS>	Address.
<BLOCKQUOTE>...</BLOCKQUOTE>	Block quote. PageMill calls this Indent Right.

List Tags

<UL><LI>...</UL> — Unordered (bullet) list.

<UL TYPE=disc|circle|square><LI>...</UL> — Unordered list with type of bullet specified. [2]

<LI TYPE=disc|circle|square> — Type of bullet for list item. [2]

<OL><LI>...</OL> — Ordered (numbered) list.

<OL TYPE=A\a\I\i\1><LI>...</OL> — Ordered list with type of outline scheme specified. [2]

<LI TYPE=A\a\I\i\1> — Outline scheme for ordered list item. [2]

<OL VALUE=#><LI>...</OL> — Ordered list with starting number specified. [2]

<LI VALUE=#> — Starting number for ordered list item. [2]

<DL><DT>...<DD>...</DL> — Definition list.

<MENU><LI>...</MENU> — Menu list.

<DL><LI>...</DL> — Directory list.

Image Tags

<IMG SRC="url"> — Display image at specified URL.

<IMG SRC="url" ALIGN=top|bottom|middle> — Display image with specified alignment.

<IMG SRC="url" ALT="text"> — Display image and define alternate text.

<IMG SRC="url" ISMAP> — Display image and define it as an image map.

<IMG SRC="url" WIDTH=# HEIGTH=#> — Display image with the specified height and width.

<IMG SRC="url" BORDER=#> — Display image with the specified border width.

<IMG SRC="url" HSPACE=# VSPACE=#> — Display image with runaround space. [2]

<IMG SRC="url" LOWSRC="url"> — Display image and specify low-resolution proxy image. [2]

Link Tags

<A HREF="url"></A> — Link to specified URL.

<A HREF="#anchor" — Link to specified anchor.

<A HREF="url#anchor" — Link to specified anchor on specified URL.

<A NAME="anchor"></A> — Define anchor.

<BASE HREF="url"> — Specify absolute URL base to be used for relative links. Must be the complete pathname for the current page. [1]

<LINK REV="relation" REL="relation" HREF="url"> — Specifies a relationship between the current URL and another one. [1]

Form Tags

<FORM ACTION="url" METHOD=get|post></FORM> — Define form.

<INPUT TYPE="text|password|checkbox|radio|submit|reset"> — Input field type.

<INPUT NAME="name"> — Input field name.

<INPUT VALUE="value"> — Input field value.

<INPUT CHECKED> — Checked input field.

<INPUT SIZE=#> — Input field size, in characters

<INPUT MAXLENGTH=#> — Input field maximum length, in characters.

<SELECT></SELECT> — Selection list.

<SELECT NAME="name"></SELECT> — Selection list name.

<SELECT SIZE=#></SELECT> — Selection list number of options.

<SELECT MULTIPLE> — Selection list with multiple selections allowed.

<OPTION> — Selection list option.

<OPTION SELECTED> — Default option in a selection list.

<TEXTAREA ROWS=# COLS=#></TEXTAREA> — Text area size.

<TEXTAREA NAME="name"></TEXTAREA> — Text area name.

Table Tags

<TABLE>...</TABLE> Define table. [3]

<TABLE BORDER>...</TABLE> Define table with a border. [3]

<TABLE BORDER=#>...</TABLE> Define table with a specified border thickness. [2]

<TABLE CELLSPACING=#>...</TABLE>
Define table with specified space between cells. [2]

<TABLE CELLPADDING=#>...</TABLE>
Define table with specified additional space within cells. [2]

<TABLE WIDTH=#>...</TABLE> Define table of specified width. [2]

<TABLE WIDTH=#%>...</TABLE> Define table of specified width expressed in percent of window width. [2]

<TR>...</TR> Table row. [3]

<TR ALIGN=left|right|center>...</TR>
Table row with horizontal alignment within cells specified. [3]

<TR VALIGN=top|middle|bottom>...</TR>
Table row with vertical alignment within cells specified. [3]

<TH>...</TH> Table header. [3]

<TH ALIGN=left|right|center>...</TH>
Table header with horizontal alignment within cell specified. [3]

<TH VALIGN=top|middle|bottom>...</TH>
Table header with vertical alignment within cell specified. [3]

<TH NOWRAP>...</TH> Table header with word wrap within the cell turned off. [3]

<TH COLSPAN=#>...</TH> Table header with column span specified. [3]

<TH ROWSPAN=#>...</TH> Table header with row span specified. [3]

<TH WIDTH=#>...</TH> Table header with width of cell specified. [2]

<TH WIDTH=#%>...</TH> Table header with width of cell specified in terms of a percent of the table width. [2]

<TD>...</TD> Table cell. [3]

<TD ALIGN=left|right|center>...</TD>
Table cell with horizontal alignment within cell specified. [3]

<TD VALIGN=top|middle|bottom>...</TD>	Table cell with vertical alignment within cell specified. [3]
<TD NOWRAP>...</TD>	Table cell with word wrap within the cell turned off. [3]
<TD COLSPAN=#>...</TD>	Table cell with column span specified. [3]
<TD ROWSPAN=#>...</TD>	Table cell with row span specified. [3]
<TD WIDTH=#>...</TD>	Table cell with width of cell specified. [2]
<TD WIDTH=#%>...</TD>	Table cell with width of cell specified in terms of a percent of the table width. [2]
<CAPTION>...</CAPTION>	Table caption. [3]
<CAPTION ALIGN=top|bottom>...</CAPTION>	Table caption with location specified. [3]

Special Character Tags

&lt	<
&gt	>
&amp	&
&quot	"
&reg	®
&copy	©

Notes

1 Although supported by PageMill, these tags cannot be applied using PageMill's menu commands or other options. You must enter them manually and format them as Raw HTML.

2 Netscape extensions to HTML 2.0.

3 HTML 3.0 markup tags.

INDEX

Index

Index

O

P

Q

R

S

T

U

V

W

Z